WEST LAVINGTON VILLAC

Snippets from the Past

by

Lyn Dyson

All proceeds from the sale of this book will go to:

The West Lavington Youth Club

Registered Charity No 1080380

From the Author

While researching a specific incident in Lavington history, I took out a subscription to the British Newspaper Archive, and immediately found myself totally immersed in events which happened in our villages.

I tried to concentrate on West Lavington, but did occasionally stray into neighbouring villages. One of my early discoveries was of the Lavington Imposter, who is deservedly the subject of a separate book all to himself. But I have since found cases of agricultural strikes in West Lavington, even before the time of the Tolpuddle Martyrs who are credited with forming the first trade union; arson, poisoning and abduction, all happening within our neighbourhood during the Victorian age.

This volume doesn't pretend to cover all the reported events in West Lavington during the 19th century, but I hope I have managed to find some of the more interesting ones. If you are squeamish, you may not wish to read the section on inquest reports, but if you have ancestors who lived here, you may well find them interesting. It is very sad to see how many young children died when their clothing caught fire. Thank goodness we have fire guards and less flammable fabrics these days.

We talk a lot about climate change, but the weather cropped up frequently as a news item one-hundred-and-fifty years ago as well, with tales of enormous hail stones or massive amounts of snow, and lightning strikes etc.

The newspaper reports of the day had their own colourful language, and I have tried to retain that here. I could just have rewritten it as a narrative, but to be honest, I think the reporters of the day did it better. Or at least, they did it their way, and I see nothing wrong with preserving that. I wish I knew who they were!!!

Anyway, as I can't personally acknowledge the authors, my thanks must go to the British Newspaper Archive and the British Library for allowing me to publish the text of the reports. They hold all the rights to these articles. They have mostly come from the Devizes and Wiltshire Gazette, with the occasional contribution from the Salisbury Journal and the Wiltshire Independent.

The cover photograph has kindly been supplied by Market Lavington Museum, and shows the Box family at their home at Broadway House, now Mowbray House. It was taken some years after the incident related in Chapter Nine.

Other photographs in this book are with kind permission from Ros Hooper.

I am grateful to Keira Michelle Telford for all her help in getting this volume into print.

All proceeds from the sale of this book go to West Lavington Youth Club. Thank you for purchasing it.

Lyn Dyson
West Lavington
01380 813943
lyndadyson@yahoo.co.uk
October 1012

Illustrations

Fig 1. The Wiltshire Friendly Society meeting at the Wheatsheaf Inn.

Fig 2. Potters Bus at Market Lavington.

Fig 3. The Box Family at Broadway House (now called Mowbray House).

Contents

Chapter One
Snippets from the Past

6th March 1823

The Black Dog public house in the parish of West Lavington was consumed by fire on Saturday last. It was supposed to have originated in the chimney from whence it proceeded to the thatch, thence to every part of the house, and continuing with great fury from between 7 and 8 until 12 o'clock, the stock of beer and casks together with the furniture as well as the house was entirely destroyed. The house was insured in the Salamander Fire Office, and the stock in the Norwich Union.

25th December 1823

On Friday sennight a splendid fete was celebrated at Wychwood Lodge, Oxon, the seat of Lord Churchill, in honour of his lordship's eldest son, the Hon Francis George Spencer, coming of age. The nobility and gentry of the vicinity were all present. His lordship partook of the hospitable celebrity, and the day was closed by a ball, which was opened by the Hon Miss Spencer and the Hon Mr Dillon. At West Lavington the tenantry and their families were also entertained by a ball and a supper.

July 1825

Between 3 and 4 o'clock in the morning of Friday last, a fire, which had made some progress before it was discovered, broke out in the house of Mr William Draper of Lavington. The inmates were in bed and asleep; but fortunately the string by which a warming pan hung, was burnt, and the noise occasioned by the falling of the pan aroused Mr Draper to a sense of the danger that surrounded him. But for this providential circumstance, the house in all probability would very shortly have been enveloped in flames, when no human power could have prevented its extending to the number of thatched cottages adjoining. Mr Draper procured assistance, and it was extinguished without doing any very serious injury.

29th May 1834

Devizes Petty Sessions

There were several cases of assault and battery arising from the frolics of Whitsuntide. In one of these, a young man from Lavington charged another young man with biting off the top joint of one of his fingers. The defendant pleaded a justification, on the ground that the finger was violently and feloniously thrust into his mouth for the purpose of stealing some part of the contents of the said mouth, namely, the tongue or certain of the teeth; and that the defendant in order to prevent such depredation did in his self-defence, demolish that part of the said finger only which was so sacrilegiously thrust into his mouth; and thereupon issue was joined. A great number of witnesses were examined, pro and con, and it was clearly proved that in a dispute, the complainant by some means did put his finger into the mouth of the defendant, although not with felonious intent pleaded; and it was also proved that when the said finger was taken from the mouth of the defendant, it was minus the top joint. The Magistrates appeared to think that there ought to be some tax put upon such an unnatural appetite as the defendant had evinced, but they deferred giving their opinion as to the amount of that tax until the next meeting.

25th March 1837

Died on 13th December last, at Kamptee in the East indies, aged 28, Mr William Henderson of the East India Company's Artillery, youngest son of C R Henderson Esq. of West Lavington House, near Devizes, leaving a widow and an infant daughter only three weeks old. Respected and esteemed by his officers, his promotion in the East India Army has been rapid, and beloved by his comrades, he was buried amidst their regret, with a soldier's honours, and in a soldier's grave.

(C. R. Henderson was the steward or agent for Lord Churchill, and was responsible for the administration of the Estate in West Lavington.)

8th November 1838

Three Guineas Reward

Absconded from West Lavington about twelve months since, and left his wife and family chargeable to that parish, Robert Lane, about 35 years of age, 5ft 9 inches high, dark swarthy complexion and round featured.

A REWARD OF THREE GUINEAS, with all reasonable expenses, will be paid to any person who will bring him to the Overseers of West Lavington. He is supposed to be working on the Great Western Railway, and was seen last summer in the neighbourhood of Box.

(Robert Lane was born in Great Cheverell in 1803, and was married to Sarah Slade. At the time of this notice, they had two children: Robert, aged 8, and Sarah, aged 3. Robert must have been found because the family was reunited and they continued to live at Great Cheverell.)

7th March 1839

A Tale of Salisbury Plain
(Wiltshire Independent)
(from a correspondent)

In passing over the vast downs of Salisbury Plain from Lavington to Chittern, the traveller may notice a long line of heaps of chalk, placed at regular intervals and reaching the whole of the distance between these two places. On enquiry as to the origin of this line, I was much entertained with the following story:

Some years ago, a gentleman residing at Chittern paid his addresses to a very fascinating young lady at Lavington, whose attractions were frequently the cause of his having to cross the downs at a very late hour. On one of these occasions, being unusually late, he found that though 'the course of true love' was in his case tolerably *smooth,* it was by no means *straight;* for after wandering about during the whole of a most miserable night, he found himself in the morning, only a mile or two from the place whence he had set out on the previous evening. To prevent the recurrence of a similar misfortune- he had a quantity of chalk placed at such distances, so that even in the darkest night it would be easy to trace his way across the grassy Hellespont in safety. The heaps are now somewhat overgrown with moss and grass, but for years to come, the traveller will have reason to thank Mr_____, or rather the attractions of his lady, for a most useful clue to the road from Lavington to Chittern.

3rd October 1839

Wiltshire Independent

Salisbury Plain: Our readers will recollect that a few months since we gave the history of a line of heaps of chalk, extending across the Downs from Lavington to Chittern, which were placed by an erratic lover to guide him home after his visits to his adored. We have just been informed by a correspondent that a direction post has lately been erected on the Downs midway between Chittern and Tilshead bearing the following inscription:

To Tilshead ←→ To Chittern
To Lavington, Keep by the Chalk Heaps.

These heaps of chalk would become doubly useful were a post erected at Gore Cross, where several roads meet, and have on it the following direction: To Tilshead, to Imber, to Chittern, Keep by the Chalk Heaps.

5th August 1841

Providential Escape

On Friday last, Mr Thomas of the White Lion Inn in Devizes, attended the Bean Feast at the Black Dog Inn, West Lavington, and when about to leave, he put up his stick for the purpose of unhooking his hat. Near his hat a gun was suspended, by some unsound cord, and as the stick accidentally touched the cord the gun fell and exploded, the contents of which passed through one of the flaps of Mr Thomas' coat, and took away a portion of the brim of his hat on the opposite side without even touching his person.

A more singular escape from serious injury, if not from death, perhaps was never heard of. It might be considered impossible that the contents of the gun could pass so without injury.

The person to whom the gun belonged must have shown great carelessness, to say the least of it, in allowing a loaded gun to be so suspended.

15th May 1845

The number of deaths registered for the quarter ending in March has in most districts exceeded the average. At Lavington there were 49 deaths, 5 arising from typhus fever and 3 from whooping cough. There were more than the usual mortality among the aged, 18 having died above the age of 60 years; no less than 4 coroner's inquests were held in this district during the quarter.

11th December 1845

We regret to learn that the inconvenience consequent on Lord Radnor's new plan of letting his farms by tender and refusing to give the old tenants the option of continuing their occupation on fair and equitable terms in the

Lavington district, is not confined to the larger tenants. Many of the poor in the tithing of Littleton who had rented allotments under his lordship's direction, from the time of the agricultural riots in 1830, are now, to their sorrow, deprived of them.

13th August 1846

Caution to Corn Dealers Attending Devizes Market

There was a law in place which required anyone purchasing corn to complete a return within one week of the purchase and hand it to the Inspector appointed by the Act. It was established that as many as 15 or 16 corn dealers attending the market in Devizes had submitted no returns in the previous year and a half. The Excise Officer was considered to be partly to blame for allowing the matter to continue unchecked. However the situation was about to be rectified.

The first case to be highlighted was Mr Amram Saunders, miller of West Lavington. Mr Spencer of Lavington proved that he had sold 56 sacks of wheat for £72.11.6d to Mr Saunders in January 1846 and no return had been made.

Mr Saunders said he was so ignorant of the Act that he did not know there were any penalties attached to non-compliance with its provisions. He never had any objection to making the return, but the truth was he frequently felt so fatigued after the business of the market that he did not feel inclined to go across to the Bear Inn and deliver his return to the Inspector. If he had been well and strong he would have made it. He admitted that he might occasionally have forgotten it, due to the multitude of business he had to transact, but it was his wish to make it. He said it would be very convenient if he could have the papers at home so that he could fill them out on his return from market, and deliver them the following week.

The Magistrates accepted that Mr Saunders had failed to submit the return in error, and that as this was the first case brought under the Act, the penalty of a fine of £20 was to be mitigated to £5. The Magistrates pointed out that a much heavier fine would be ordered in the event of any future offences.

Mr Saunders paid the fine and the expenses of £2.2.6d.

7th December 1846

Letter to the Editor

Mr Editor,

May I request you to insert in your paper, the rules of a club established in this parish about two and half years since, for the destruction of sparrows.

It is supported by voluntary contributions, and a regular account kept of receipts and expenditure. 3d per dozen heads is allowed during the summer half year; 4d per dozen during the winter half. Each receiver's name, and money paid is entered from time to time, and the book is open for inspection of the subscribers. Each allotment tenant is expected to produce one dozen sparrows yearly, or forfeit 2d at the rent day. By this plan no less than 10,572 sparrows have been destroyed during the time the club has been in operation; and my object in inviting the attention of neighbouring parishes to this fact is that general co-operation throughout the district may more effectually secure the object proposed; a most desirable one, especially where the allotment system prevails, and the damage done by small birds is doubly felt.

I remain, Sir, your humble obedient servant,
James Ingram, Overseer of West Lavington.

20ᵗʰ May 1847

Dreadful Death

Yesterday morning a boy about 11 years of age named Stiles, of West Lavington, was found burnt to death in a limekiln belonging to his father. He had it appears gone out for the purpose of feeding his father's horse, but being absent longer than usual, a search was made for him and his body was at length found in his father's lime kiln.

(This was Thomas Stiles, or more probably, Stills. He was the son of lime burner John Stills and his wife Maria. They lived around Stibb Hill.)

2ⁿᵈ December 1847

Following eight or nine months of restoration, the Church at West Lavington was re-opened for Divine Service.

The church was originally an early English structure, built probably in the commencement of the 13ᵗʰ century. What alterations it underwent in earlier times is unknown, but it certainly was once a church of much beauty, and considerable pains had been taken with its decoration. This appears from one or two small fragments that have been found of encaustic tiles, mouldings with rich painting and gilding etc. However at a later period the church had been so completely torn to pieces, in a great measure by violent means, square house windows having been substituted for the early lancet; the mouldings etc having been broken into small fragments, and built into the walls, that few features remained of its original appearance. Decay and neglect and ignorance almost completed the work, and thus this fine church, at the beginning of the year, presented the appearance of a dilapidated structure, with galleries disfiguring the arches, with a flat roof and sky lights, the clerestory windows being blocked up, square pews and other unsightly appearances.

The work was commenced in the month of April and the church has now been restored as nearly as possible to what it may be supposed was its original design. The proportions are admirable. The south transept, having been converted into a sort of mausoleum for the family of the lord of the manor in former days, has been given up by Lord Churchill for the use of the congregation. It is now seated uniformly with the rest of the church, and by these means an increase of 200 sittings has been gained, notwithstanding the demolition of the galleries. The space in the tower too has been thrown into the church, and seated for a girl's school. The font, which is the original one, stands under the western arch. This portion of the church was entirely lost and obscured by the galleries. The style throughout is early English, with the exception of the vestry and the Dauntsey aisle, or south transept, which have not been altered as to their architectural appearance. They are very good perpendicular.

The church has been entirely re-roofed, and the roof of the nave has been restored to its original pitch. It is constructed of oak, we believe after the model of the cathedral of Ely, confessedly one of the finest timber roofs in the kingdom. The choral roof is of oak panelling, with intersecting ribs and bosses at the angles, the ribs and bosses being painted and gilt. The altar is of exquisite design and workmanship, composed of an arcade of Early English arches with richly carved capitals in oak. The east window, by Ward and Nixon is rich with dim religious light, the colouring being harmoniously blended in a pattern of early English character, with a medallion in the centre light containing a beautiful group representing the Ascension of our Blessed Lord. The north transept and western windows are by Powell, and are very creditable specimens of his skill. There is also a beautiful small Early English window by Powell in the east gable of the nave above the Chancel arch which has a peculiarly fine effect, relieving the spaces of plain work, which would otherwise have been unsightly.

The prayer desk and lectern are of well carved oak, and with the chancel stalls, as well indeed as the whole of the woodwork in the church, are most creditable to the workmen employed upon them. The seats are low, of oak, uniform and open, yet most comfortably arranged. In short, without entering into further detail of the work that has been accomplished, we may say with truth that there are few village churches in this diocese presenting an interior altogether so harmonious in style and adornment as that of West Lavington. Everything is in keeping; substantial yet beautiful with seemly decorations; handsome yet quiet and sober withal.

Altogether we can believe Tuesday last to have been a proud day to the Vicar and his parishioners; and what added to the interesting proceedings of the occasion was the christening of the infant daughter of the rev, incumbent, by the Bishop, during the morning service. Hospitality reigned throughout the village, almost every house that could afford it was opened to guests, with a true Wiltshire hearty welcome, and the day was made one of general rejoicing.

The expense of the completed work will, it is hoped, not amount to more than £1600, but we understand that not more than £1400 has yet been contributed. The sum has been raised partly by rate (£500); Lord Churchill and the Bishop of the Diocese also contributing largely, and the former having expressed his wish to add £100 to his former gift of £200, in order that the tower might be repaired. The Church Societies have also come forward. In short there has been no lack of zeal or generosity.

14th December 1848

Chippenham Agricultural Society

The premiums offered by R J Holford Esq. were awarded to James Kite of West Lavington, who has a family of eight children respectably brought up without parochial assistance, except on one or two occasions when the children had the fever and the measles.

(This was James Kite, born in 1809 in Tilshead. He married Elizabeth Bundy in 1831, and the couple settled in West Lavington around 1836. They had 9 children altogether, the last one being born in 1853. They lived in White Street.)

28th December 1848

A serious accident happened at West Lavington on Tuesday last. A party had been shooting for a dinner at the Lamb Inn, when a gun burst, and a portion of the barrel came with great force against the head of a young man named James Chapman. The poor fellow immediately fell insensible to the ground, and although he is still alive, there is no hope of his recovery. (He is since dead).

(James Chapman was the son of labourer William Chapman and his wife Mary. He was 26 years old when he died.)

24th May 1849

The village of West Lavington was the scene of much joyous festivity on Saturday last, in consequence of the celebration of the marriage of the Right Hon. Lord Churchill with the Lady Jane Conyngham, daughter of the Marquess Of Conyngham, as reported in our marriages of this week. His Lordship had kindly directed a very liberal distribution of beef, bread, and beer amongst the poorer inhabitants. These orders were duly, and with much orderly arrangement, carried into effect, under the superintendence of Mr Kelsey, the steward of the West Lavington estates; and above 230 families were thus enabled to participate in the general joy felt in an event so immediately connected with the happiness of one of the most respected of our Wiltshire nobility. During the day the village bells sent forth many merry peals, and the band paraded the streets, playing lively airs, and attended by a large assemblage of the happy participants in the good cheer just dealt out to them. In the evening a grand display of fireworks took place from one of the commanding hills above West Lavington, which was highly creditable to the skill and taste of Mr Withers, the artist supplying them: It is computed that more than 3000 people were assembled to witness the exhibition, which would have afforded perfect satisfaction had not the evening proved so unpropitious. His Lordship and his fair bride arrived at West Lavington House on Monday evening, and will make some sojourn there. We are persuaded that his presence amongst a most respectable tenantry, and a well-conducted, orderly population, employed chiefly on the estates of which his Lordship is the liberal and highly esteemed proprietor, will be hailed with sincere pleasure, and contribute much to strengthen those feelings of grateful respect which have ever been entertained by the inhabitants of West Lavington towards that excellent and distinguished family of which his Lordship now is, and we trust may for many happy years continue to be, the worthy and honoured representative.

11th October 1849

Cholera Epidemic

The Bishop of Salisbury sanctioned a day of fasting and humiliation on October 5th, on account of a cholera epidemic.

Market Lavington and West Lavington: Friday October 5th was kept in these parishes as a day of solemn fasting and humiliation, on account of the pestilence prevailing throughout the country. As in all other parishes of which we have heard where such a day has been appointed, it was most reverently and devoutly observed. The shops were closed; the farmers, with one consent, gave the day up to their labourers, and the inhabitants, with hardly an exception, seemed anxious to acknowledge the hand by which the chastisement has been inflicted, and with all humility to confess their dependence upon God, and pray Him to abate the distemper. The parish churches were crowded, both morning and evening, and all seemed most devoutly to recognise and enter into the intention and solemnity of the day.

27th March 1851

On Tuesday, a young man named Rumble of West Lavington who had been to Rowde in search of work, was returning homewards when he met with Mr Hooper's carter, with whom he went into a beer-house at Potterne and had some beer, being at the same time quite tipsy. He then got on the waggon to ride, but after going about a mile, he made an attempt to get off, and in doing so he fell, and both wheels passed over him. He was immediately conveyed home, and died a few hours later.

(This was William Rumble, the son of agricultural labourer Henry, and Elizabeth Rumble. He was 20 years of age when he died.)

25th September 1851

A shocking accident happened to a labouring man named Shore at West Lavington on Friday last. A man who was attending a thrashing machine, which was at work upon Mr Hulbert's farm, had occasion to leave for a few minutes, when Shore offered to take his place, and was striding across a portion of the machinery for the purpose of doing so, when his foot became entangled in the works, and in an instant his leg was completely smashed. He was immediately conveyed home and a surgeon sent for, when his mangled limb was amputated, but the poor fellow died the following morning.

(This was Moses Shore, born in 1826, the son of labourer William and Leah Shore. He was 25 years old.)

On Monday, as the mother and sisters of the deceased were returning through Potterne from Devizes, between 8 and 9 o'clock in the evening, the conveyance in which they were riding came into contact with another carriage which was passing the church corner, and both vehicles were upset. The parties however fortunately escaped with a few bruises.

5th August 1852

West Lavington: On Friday last, one of Hussey's American Reaping Machines, 'improved', was started by Mr Silcock of Chippenham, on the farm of Mr William Hooper of West Lavington. And as it is, we believe, one of the first that has been put into regular use in this county, a short account of the way in which it performed its work may be interesting.

For convenience the trial was as private as possible, and made purposely to test the actual capabilities of the machine. It was first started on a piece of ripe rye, which was very much lodged; so much so that Mr Hooper remarked that if it would cut that cleanly it would cut or reap almost anything. At first, a little difficulty was experienced in raking the straw off the platform, owing to the men not being accustomed to it, and to their being rather too hasty. But this difficulty was soon overcome as the men got more used to the work, and the straw was then laid off regularly, in proper quantities for tying up.

The machine worked admirably, going through the grain whether lodged or not in first rate style, and leaving stubble within about four inches of the ground, as clean and level on the top as a newly mown grass-plat. And although in many places there was a quantity of Italian rye grass on the ground, it cut through all without clogging, thus proving its capability of cutting green grass as well as grain, wherever the ground is at all adapted for using it. When at regular work, it cut at the rate of nearly an acre and a half an hour.

June 1857

Caution to the Benevolent

Two men, one dressed in a decent white smock frock, and having the appearance of a dairyman, called upon several gentlemen at West Lavington last week, with a petition setting forth that Mrs Watts of Corsley, near Warminster, had recently lost nine very valuable cows from disease. Several we learn, readily contributed a few shillings; but upon the Rev Mr Wilton writing to the clergyman of Corsley respecting the alleged loss, he was informed by return of post that the whole tale was a hoax. We trust the police will soon be enabled to stop the career of the rascals.

July 1857

A party of young labouring men were summoned by the police constable of West Lavington for resisting the police in endeavouring to put down what is popularly known as a 'skimating', or 'Skimmington'. The affair did not appear to be accompanied with the indecencies which frequently attend such exhibitions, nor did there appear to have been any mischief resulting from the noise and clamour with which the demonstration was celebrated. But the police considered that a breach of the peace might arise from it and they very properly endeavoured to put a stop to it, and summoned the parties who resisted them in their endeavours; each of whom was fined 1 shilling and dismissed with a caution as to respecting similar displays. Those who were charged with resisting the police were:

William Baker; Richard Potter, a farm labourer born in 1835; Richard Bundy, a market gardener born in 1835; Robert Coleman, a farmer born in 1834; Henry Dark, an agricultural labourer who died in Fiddington Lunatic Asylum in 1860; James Gough, an agricultural labourer born in 1833; Joseph Nutland, a gardener born in 1837; William Nutland, a miller born in 1831; George Topp (also known as George Phillips).

(Skimating, or skimmington, was an old custom of publicly humiliating a man or a woman who was believed to have been unfaithful to his or her spouse. They would process down the street, banging on pots and pans, singing rude songs and carrying some graphic images or effigies. Whilst it was mainly done to humiliate an unfaithful wife or husband, it was sometimes arranged to humiliate a cuckolded man who accepted his wife's adultery.)

7th January 1858

Half a fat ox and a suitable quantity of potatoes, the liberal gift of W. Beckett-Turner Esq., were yesterday distributed among the poor of the tithing of Littleton Panell in West Lavington. The vicar of West Lavington and Mr Abraham Newman kindly superintended the distribution of Mr Beckett-Turner's bounty, which we need scarcely say, was received with grateful hearts by the poor. We may add that Mr Turner has, within the last two years, very handsomely given £50 towards the school of the parish.

22nd July 1858

A serious accident happened to Mr T. Neate of West Lavington a few days ago as he was returning from Devizes. He was driving in a four wheel carriage when the horse, from some cause took fright, overturned the vehicle and threw Mr Neate upon the road with such violence that his leg was broken. We are happy to hear however that he is proceeding favourably towards recovery.

(Thomas Neate was from Pyt House in Duck Street.)

28th October 1858

A dreadful and distressing accident occurred near Market Lavington between 6 and 7 o'clock on Tuesday evening, resulting in the death of Mr William Gye of Fiddington. He was returning from Warminster fair, in a light spring waggon, accompanied by Mr Thomas Draper and Mr John

Hopkins, when in descending the hill from Littleton to Lavington, near the spot where the little boy was killed two months since, the horse shied, and ran the wheels on the bank at the side of the road, by which the waggon was turned on its side, and Mr Gye was instantly killed. He was respected throughout the neighbourhood, and his untimely end is deeply lamented. He has left a wife and four children.

(William Gye farmed 50 acres at Fiddington. He was married to Sophia, and they were both aged 50 when William was killed. Sophia continued to run the farm.)

13th January 1859

West Lavington: During this winter the Rev Dr Wilkinson has succeeded in establishing a course of penny lectures at the large schoolroom, for the benefit of the working classes; and lectures of a highly interesting character have been delivered by various clergymen of the neighbourhood. Last evening there was a musical entertainment by amateurs, and the room was thronged for the occasion, upwards of 500 persons being present. The selection of music was good, and the performance highly creditable to the ladies and gentlemen who took part in it, who were Mrs and Miss E Hitchcock, Mrs Kelsey, the Misses Caswell (Devizes), Miss Fishlake, Miss Hooper, Miss Wilkinson, and Mrs Neate, Mr Neate, Mr Loyd, and the Rev Mr Cleather of Marden.

20th January 1859

Some few years ago, a poor woe-stricken man named John Bartlett, having tried to procure himself a wife in his own parish without effect, presented himself at the door of the Devizes Union Workhouse, and earnestly entreated the Mistress to get him one from among the inmates of the house. The Mistress took compassion upon him, assembled all the young women together, and plainly put the question, "Who is for a husband and Australia?" telling them that a man at the door awaited their answer.

"I am!" immediately exclaimed Sarah Eardley. "And first speak, first chance!" she said. What she said was law to the inmates, and she had power to enforce her law; she was six feet high, had six toes upon each foot, and was possessed of corresponding strength.

Sarah was at the door in a twinkle, and having momentarily surveyed her man, she said "I am your match!"

"Then pick up your traps!" said he, and within ten minutes Sarah Eardley was walking out of Devizes traps in hand, an affianced bride.

They were married, but did not as first intended proceed to Australia. She led John a sorry time of it, and has played many a part on the stage of life. She has occasionally returned to her old quarters in the Union, and has headed a storming party against the Master's windows; has wreaked vengeance upon the porter by stripping his head of its hair, besides divers other matters.

She is now, however, safely lodged in the New Prison on a charge of burglary, which it is alleged she committed in company with a relative named Ann Eardley. It appears that as Mr Noad of Potterne was returning home about half past 12 on Monday night, he saw two women standing at his home-field gate, who on his approach ran off in different directions. He soon overtook Ann, and identified her, she having left his service about a week ago.

Leaving Ann he pursued Sarah, but she was too nimble for him, and escaped. Proceeding to his house he found the back door, the cheese room door, and a window open, and two cheeses, a pair of boots, and other articles were missing. He gave information to the police, and Sarah was apprehended before day-break at her own house in

Lavington; and Ann shortly afterwards at the railway station at Trowbridge, on her road to Bath, where she had obtained a situation. They were brought before the Magistrates today, and committed for trial.

(Sarah Earley was born in Erlestoke in 1829. She had a daughter, Mary Ann Earley, born in 1848 in Devizes. Mary Ann was brought up by her grandparents in Erlestoke. Sarah married George Bartlett, a hawker from West Lavington, in 1853. They lived together in White Street, West Lavington, until George's death in 1891 at the age of 66. Sarah died in 1902 at the age of 73. They had no children.)

26th May 1859

The amateur concert at West Lavington for the benefit of the School Building Fund was held yesterday evening. The programme was well chosen and the various performances reflected great credit on those who sustained them. It would be invidious to particularize any, where all did well. The ladies and gentlemen of West Lavington and neighbourhood possess no mean musical power; and on this occasion they were ably assisted by a few amateurs from other places: Mrs Fletcher, Mrs Dyson, and the Rev George Cleather.

The spacious schoolroom was well filled with a select party, and everyone present seemed delighted and surprised with the manner which the several pieces were performed.

23rd June 1859

West Lavington: On Monday the annual festival of this branch of the Wilts Friendly Society was kept. The members attended divine service in the parish church, where a most appropriate and stirring address was delivered by the Rev Prebendary Fane. They afterwards assembled at dinner in the parish schoolroom, which was tastefully decorated for the occasion, and where a most excellent repast was provided by Mr Baker of the

Wheatsheaf. There was a large attendance of benefit members, as well as honorary members and visitors, numbering in all about 130 or from that to 150.

Among the company were the Honorable Mrs Hay, Revs Prebendary Fane, Dr Wilkinson, M. W. Mayow, R. U. Lambert; Mrs Wilkinson, Mrs Mayow, Mrs Toogood, Mrs Kelsey, Mrs Lush, Misses Wilton, Miss Sainsbury, Misses Bennett, Miss Newman, Miss Fishlake, Miss Fowle, Miss Smith, Miss Wilkinson, Mr Kelsey, Mr H. Butcher, Mr A. Newman, Mr N. Hooper, Mr H. Lawes, Mr Ellis, Mr T. Butcher, Mr D. Wilkinson.

The usual toasts were given, and the dinner with its speeches passed off as such events usually do at these very agreeable meetings of all classes. The day had been showery and unpromising for out of door sports, but the sun came out, and between 4 and 5 o'clock a large party, numbering probably 700 or 800, repaired to a spacious field, kindly lent by Mr Kelsey for the purpose, where with dancing, foot races and other diversions, both body and mind were refreshed and invigorated, and about 9 o'clock 'God save the Queen' was played, and all dispersed, well satisfied and with happy hearts to their homes.

Fig. 1

15th December 1859

Chippenham Agricultural Association: The society's premium of £2 for servants is awarded to agricultural labourers who have lived the longest time with one master. On this occasion the prize went to John Toppe, servant to Mr William Sainsbury of West Lavington for 29 years.

(This was probably the John Top who was born in West Lavington in 1806. He married Mary Ellis of Market Lavington in 1829, and although their first child was born in Market Lavington the following year, the couple were living in West Lavington from at least 1832 when their next child was born. John was an agricultural labourer but by 1871 his occupation was farm bailiff. He and Mary had four children.)

27th December 1860

Chippenham Agricultural Association: The labourer's premium of £5 went to Ann Godden, servant to Mr William Sainsbury of West Lavington for 40 years servitude.

13th June 1861

On Mr Sainsbury's Farm at West Lavington: Mechanical ingenuity as applied to agricultural purposes is every day becoming a matter of increasing interest to the farmer, and with catching weather such as we have had during the last two or three summers, it is of no small importance to those who have large crops to gather in, that they should, in the words of the old adage, seize every opportunity of 'making hay while the sun shines'. Thanks to the spirit of our agricultural machinists, who, it will be fairly confessed, spare no expense to meet the times in the way of modern improvements, facilities of doing this are yearly brought forth such as the grandfathers of the present generation little dreamt of; and it must in justice be admitted that we owe much to the enterprising firms who have laboured for so many years to help the farmer in this respect, for if there be one machine more than another which is needed at such a season as this, it is a good, practical, efficient, and at the same time simple reaping and Mowing Machine. And we really believe that such a machine has at last been invented.

Mr William Sainsbury, whose name is known throughout England in connection with the Royal Agricultural Society, yesterday afforded the agriculturalists in this neighbourhood an opportunity of testing the merits of two of these most noted machines upon his farm at West Lavington, and a more satisfactory or a more interesting trial of such implements has seldom been witnessed. The spot selected for the scene of operations was Gore Cross, where we need scarcely say Mr Sainsbury had made ample provision for the hospitable reception of his friends. With preliminary fortification of some prime Wiltshire grazed beef and a glass of first rate sherry, the company about one o' clock wended their way to a large piece of clover and grass, growing a short distance off, and a splendid piece of clover and grass it was, particularly the upper part of it, which we should say might be computed at at least two tons to the acre. Here we found the machines all ready for the start, and in a few minutes Samuelson's, which was the first to go to work, was slashing the crop down with cleanness and precision, which beat all the mowing by hand we ever saw. The Burgess and Key machine was quickly by the side of its rival.

Each of the machines cut the crop as even as a lawn. The pace was about three miles an hour, at which about 8 or 10 acres might be thrown in a day; but it appeared to be rather stiff work for horses, and, in the opinion of those present, to cut that quantity, four horses would be required to relieve each other at intervals.

Many thanks are due to Mr Sainsbury for affording his agricultural friends an opportunity of judging the merits of these two candidates for public favour; as well as for his great liberality, which was not only shown in the providing of an excellent luncheon at the farm, but by the hospitable entertainment afterwards at his own house, where both parties connected with the machines were invited to dine.

1st December 1864

An accident which might have been attended with far more serious consequences than those which ensued, happened on Tuesday afternoon at West Lavington. It appears that the Rev Dr Wilkinson's carriage was proceeding through the village, having in it a gentleman, who was driving Miss Wilkinson and another lady who is on a visit to the family, when it was met by a horse which a man was riding, and which as the carriage passed, shied against the wheels with such violence as to completely overturn it. The consequence was that the occupants were all thrown into the road, and the horse galloped off with the carriage. But before it had gone far the shafts were broken and the vehicle otherwise considerably damaged. With this exception however we are glad to hear no harm was done, either to the party in the carriage or to anyone else. Miss Wilkinson, it is true, received a slight bruise in the arm, but beyond this all returned to the Vicarage safe.

28th December 1865

A singular accident occurred last Thursday afternoon to a boy named Robert Dark from West Lavington and which, but for the prompt assistance rendered by some persons on the spot, might have cost him his life. He was going down St. John's Street on his way home, with a cart load of coal, on top of which he was riding, when an empty waggon which had been run away with from the Elm Tree Inn came in violent contact with his cart, and knocked it over, the boy falling beneath it and the coal with which it was loaded. At first it was feared that fatal consequences would ensue, but although greatly injured, the boy is likely to recover.

(This was probably the Robert Dark who was born about 1846, the son of William Dark and Sarah Chapman.)

2nd August 1866

The Black Dog Bean Feast

The Lavington Black Dog Bean Feast took place on Friday last and was attended by about 30 persons who sat down to an excellent dinner, presided over by Mr Combes. The first prize for beans consisted of a handsome silver cream jug, given by Sir George Jenkinson, bart, and was won by Mr Hazell; the second prize went to Mr Blake of Easterton; the third to Mr Maslen of Devizes; the fourth to Mr Thompson of Devizes; the fifth to Mr R. Butcher, and the sixth to Mr Smith.

5th September 1868

Gun Accident

About 10 o'clock on Tuesday morning, a party of friends with Mr Hooper of Littleton House, West Lavington, started from that gentleman's house for a day of shooting. They had not gone about 400 yards before a covey of birds got up, which the party drove into a strip of potatoes; on their rising the second time, the birds flew all around the shooters, one of them flying behind young Mr Hooper, who without noticing his father was not in line with the party, fired and unfortunately sent the greater part of the charge into his father's leg. Mr Hooper was at the time standing under a hedge about 30 yards off, and his clothes being somewhat the same colour, prevented his son from so easily distinguishing him as he might otherwise have done.

At first it was thought that the shot had had a fatal effect, as Mr Hooper fell to the ground and was obliged to be carried home; but we are glad to hear that there is every prospect of his recovery.

5th June 1869

The Wiltshire Society

Included in the list of children elected for apprenticeship in April 1869 was Henry William Newman. His mother was formerly Jane Baish from West Lavington.

(Jane and her husband William Newman, a carpenter, settled in London. Henry William became a mechanical engineer.)

11th November 1869

The Electric Telegraph to Market Lavington

It is intended by the government to lay down, without delay, telegraphic wires from the Devizes Railway Station to the post office in the Market Lavington Place, and from thence to Market Lavington and to all places which have a money order office.

4th August 1870

Had the Lavington 'Aurora' been so heavily laden on Tuesday last, as we have frequently seen it on leaving Devizes station after the arrival of the mid-day train, its outside passengers on the 'Knifeboard' would have stood a fair chance of having fractured skulls and dislocated limbs; for its horses had scarcely got into a trot on their way into the Market Place, ere one of the wheels came off, and overturned the bus on its side.

Fortunately, the only passenger was an old lady who had taken an inside place, and who of course went over with the vehicle; but we are glad to learn that she sustained no injury, beyond a severe bumping and a considerable shock to the nervous system. This, however, was somewhat restored by the administration of a little stimulant, and she was able to pursue her journey.

The driver, upon finding what had happened, immediately leapt from the box and thus saved himself. And the wheel having been adjusted the bus proceeded on its way to Lavington. Considering that the vehicle is usually laden inside and out, it is fortunate the accident happened when it did. Its' occurrence will it is hoped make those who have the care of it careful that a similar casualty does not happen again.

Fig. 2

27th October 1870

On Thursday last at Bishops Lavington, an evening concert of vocal and instrumental music was given in the schoolroom of this parish, in aid of the organ fund. The performers who kindly lent their services on the occasion were for the most part amateurs, but their execution of the music entrusted to them was as highly satisfactory as the programme was attractive. The part-songs all went exceedingly well, but 'Come o'er the brook, Bessie' by Bishop found most favour with the audience, and elicited a hearty encore.

The lady soloists were Mrs Fletcher and Miss Hitchcock. The singing of the former, who accompanied herself in Weber's fine song, 'Yes, even love to fame must yield', displayed throughout the feeling of the true artiste and the execution of the accomplished vocalist. In compliance with a unanimous encore, and at the request of some of the audience, she gave as her second song, 'Haste thee, nymph', from Milton's L'Allegro. Miss Hitchcock sang both the songs allotted to her very prettily, and she gave Claribel's 'Love test', with a purity of tone and a charming naivete of expression that won her such an enthusiastic applause that she was constrained to repeat the last verse.

To the two fine songs 'Echoes' by Lindsay and Blumenthal's 'My Queen', Mr De St Croix, who possesses a very sweet tenor voice, did ample justice, and was deservedly encored for both. A like honour was accorded to Mr Kenningham, who with a bass voice of exceeding richness and rare compass, astonished his listeners with a double D, full round, and articulate as a diapason note of an organ.

To Miss Wilkinson, who ably sustained the treble part in a spirited duet of Schubert's with Mr Bambridge, the solo singers are deeply indebted for her admirable discharge of the important duty of accompanist. Of Mr Bambridge's performance of Beethoven's Moonlight Sonata it were almost superfluous to speak. But we may perhaps be permitted to say that whether in the tenderly melodious Adagio, the sprightly Allegretto, or the wonderfully brilliant and vigorous Presto, his interpretation and execution of the poet-musician's conceptions left nothing to be desired. His 'Auld Lang Syne', with original variations, brought down the house in thunders of applause. To these he responded with some more variations from his own pen, on 'Home Sweet Home', a composition that exemplified those marvellously executive powers of his left hand, which it is far more easy to admire than to describe. Mr Clarke who had obligingly consented to conduct the part-songs, was, we regret to say prevented from being present by the death of a relative. This office however Mr Bambridge, whose talents are only exceeded by his good nature, kindly undertook for him.

We must not forget to mention that the piano, a fine cottage of Broadwood's, was furnished gratuitously by Mr E Price, who on more than one similar occasion has shown himself ready to render this valuable assistance.

Among the audience we noticed the Hon Mrs Hay and party, Mrs and the Misses Cochrane, Dr and Mrs Wilkinson, Mrs Merriman, Rev G. E. Cleather and Miss Cleather, Rev T. Pearson and party, Rev A. B. and Mrs Thynne, Mr and Mrs Kelsey, Rev H. M. Fletcher, Rev J. Wardale, Dr Hitchcock, Mr Hulbert, and several friends from Devizes, including Mr and Mrs G. Sainsbury, Mr and Mrs J. Sainsbury, Miss Deane, Mr Langdon etc etc etc.

1st December 1870

Premium given by the Chippenham Agricultural Association for long and faithful servitude was awarded to Joseph Collings, servant to Mr William Hooper of West Lavington for 43 years.

(Joseph Collins was born in 1808 in Upton Lovell, and came to West Lavington following his marriage in 1829. He died in West Lavington in 1884, at the age of 76.)

4th May 1871

The Rev E. Wilton of West Lavington is, we are sorry to learn, lying in a very precarious state. He had been slightly out of health for 2-3 days and was going upstairs about 6 o'clock on Monday evening when, either from weakness or some more alarming cause, he fell backwards after he had got up 4-5 steps. He has since remained in an incoherent state.

13th May 1871

Death of the Rev E. Wilton

We regret to have to record the death of the Rev Edward Wilton, master of the Endowed School, West Lavington, to which post he was appointed in the year 1832, and he has now for many years been officiating minister of the Chapelry of Erle Stoke, where his ministrations and his earnestness in endeavouring to promote the welfare of those committed to his charge were well appreciated. As an archaeologist he was accurate and persevering, and many are the correspondents who would be ready to confess their obligations to him for valuable suggestions as well as for laborious investigations into points which required careful research and nice discrimination.

He was a complete master in heraldry, not only so as to be a most interesting companion to any who were desirous to trace the origin of the various quarterings on their old family shields, but he had a more than common knowledge of the science of blazoning arms or ensigns armorial. His store of knowledge on such matters was somewhat marvellous, and he was a valuable contributor to the pages of the original 'Gentleman's Magazine' and of the more modern 'Notes and Queries'.

The death of Mr Wilton, which took place on Thursday evening, May 4th will be much bewailed, not only by many relatives, but by a very wide circle of friends and correspondents. The funeral took place on Tuesday and was attended by several clergy, including the Rev Canon Jackson, the Rev C. E. Awdry, (Kington St. Michael), Rev S. Littlewood, Rev T. Pearson, Rev F. Alley, and Rev W. S. Nichols.

30 November 1871

Death of an Old Waterloo Veteran

Another Waterloo veteran has just passed away in the person of William Flowers, a native of Philip's Norton, but for many years a resident of West Lavington. His official papers show that he entered the army (1st regiment of Foot Guards) in the year 1800, served with 'The Duke' in the Peninsular Wars, was at the Battle of Corunna, and stood by at the dark and silent burial of the brave Sir J. Moore.

At Waterloo he was in the thickest of the fight, as the following incident will show: his right hand comrade fell mortally wounded, and on the poor soldier falling on Flowers, his left hand man enquired if he (Flowers) was hurt, and before Flowers could well answer him, he too fell; but our veteran came out of the battle untouched.

He was one of those who heard the ever memorable words of the old 'Iron Duke': 'Up Guards and at them!' In conversation he would often refer to them with much pride. Our veteran was in the service 26 years and on his discharge received a pension of 1s 2d per diem. He was very thin, but tall, standing about 6ft 2 inches, and bore an irreproachable character.

During the last two years of his life he was confined to his bed, and died in full possession of all his faculties, November 11th in the 97th year of his age, leaving a widow, who is now in the 74th year of her age, quite unprovided for.

7 December 1871

To the Editor of the Devizes Gazette, West Lavington, 4th December 1871:

Dear Sir,

I know not where you obtained the information which appeared in a paragraph of your paper last week relating to William Flower, late an inhabitant of this parish, but for the sake of accuracy I wish to state that I have every reason to believe his age was exaggerated, and other particulars seem to me creatures of the imagination.

I have known Pensioner Flower about 19 years, and I have visited him continually for the last 5 or 6 years. Neither in previous conversations, and we had many, nor during the last few years, has he ever been able to recount any particulars of his services in the Peninsula of Spain, or at Waterloo. Indeed he was singularly oblivious of where he had been, who had commanded, or what was done. His medals bore their testimony, but his own recollection was almost an entire blank.

He was a good old man, a communicant of the Church, and I had a great regard for him. His memory was however very defective, and especially concerning his own age. Your account and his coffin plate state him to have died at the age of 97. I am fully persuaded this is in excess of the truth by about 10 years. He was baptized on 21st October 1781 at Norton St Philip and at his death was probably in his 88th year.

Believe me,
Yours Faithfully,
M. Wilkinson.

(William Flower was buried on 15th November 1871, and his age is recorded as 87 in the parish register. This ties in with his baptism in Norton St Philip on 31st October 1784. He was married to Martha Mead in West Lavington in 1847, when he was 63 years of age, and Martha was 43. He was a widower and she was a widow. His occupation at that time was that of labourer.)

30th November 1871

Serious Accident by Fire

Last week a little girl, aged 8 years, daughter of John Boulter, a day labourer, during her mother's unavoidable absence, was blowing the fire, when a spark flew out on her dress and she was immediately engulfed in flames. The poor child ran out of the back door, when a neighbour, Mrs Potter, by wrapping her in a tick close at hand, succeeded in extinguishing the fire, but not till her neck, breast and arms were fearfully burnt.

The poor child under the care of Mr Pepler, surgeon, is doing as well as may be expected considering the sad injuries she has sustained.

(The child was Agnes Bolter, the daughter of John and Sarah Bolter, agricultural labourers living in Church Street, Market Lavington. The neighbour who rescued Agnes, was Martha Potter, a dressmaker who lived next door. Agnes never married, although she did have a daughter, Emily, born in 1896 when Agnes was 32 years of age. She didn't work, but lived with her parents, and then with her widowed mother. The 1911 census shows Agnes as working as a school caretaker. This was the first record of employment for her through all the census records).

8th March 1883

Child Burnt to Death at Lavington

A little boy, the son of Mr Goodman of the Wheatsheaf, West Lavington, was playing with matches whilst in bed on Sunday morning, when the bedclothes caught fire, and he was so seriously burnt that he died on Tuesday.

(This was Daniel Goodman, aged 3 years.)

3rd June 1883

How the Women of Lavington Let the Wife-Beater Have It
To the Editor of the Devizes Gazette:

Sir,

Our usually quiet orderly little town was the scene of a rather sensational episode on Saturday night last. It appears that some time ago a young man hailing from the neighbouring village of 'U-shant' (Urchfont) married a Lavington lass, but the union has been productive of anything but happiness. His ill treatment reached such a climax on the evening in question (the blows being heard nearly 20 yards from the house) that the poor woman screamed "murder," and thereby attracted the attention of a large number of inhabitants of the town, who all expressed the greatest indignation at the husband's conduct. The females especially gave free vent to their feelings and threatened how they would serve him if they could get hold of him, when he rather incautiously ventured too near the open door of the cottage.

He was instantly seized and dragged into the middle of the road, where half a dozen muscular females let him have it right and left. Right gallantly did the ladies of Lavington stand up for the honour of their sex, and punched away at his prostrate form until they were tired; one pugilistic female exclaiming, "Oh dear! I've been and hit my thumb out!" Another meanwhile disdaining to knock her hands to pieces, vigorously applied her foot to his person with such precision, rapidity and force, as to render the action of sitting down rather painful for some time to come.

The unfortunate recipient of all these attentions meanwhile lay unresistingly in the road in a state of apparent stupor, but the application of a bucketful of aqua pura quickly revived him.

Doubtless dreading a repetition of the dose, he sprung to his feet and made a dash for his bedroom, where he was found a few minutes later by two of the more humane among the male portion of the spectators, who gently and tenderly undressed him and put him to bed, weeping bitter tears, either of repentance for his folly or because of his inability to punish those who had so severely punished him.

It is to be hoped, Mr Editor, that the lesson which the ladies of Lavington inculcated will be a salutary warning to despotic husbands; it is at all events, a lesson which will not readily be effaced from the memory of the person to whom it was applied.

I am, Sir, One who witnessed the Flagellation.
Market Lavington, June 3rd 1883.

7th June 1883

To the Editor of the Devizes Gazette:

Sir,

In attending the Magistrates' meeting at Devizes on Monday week last, I was struck with the number of cases summoned for allowing cattle to stray, or rather bait, upon the lanes and highways. And it seems to me that the recent Act of Parliament under which they are summoned is being worked injudiciously and much too rigorously, causing an uncomfortable feeling of oppression in the breasts of many a hard working family, who find it hard to live, and very hard to be treated as criminals for appropriating the waste materials on the banks to produce a little milk for their families or a little butter for the market, and this the more especially since the Lords of the Manors have appropriated to their private use every inch of spare ground upon which many of them can well remember having the right, or at any rate the opportunity, of pasture.

The sides and banks of our lanes and highways really produce a considerable quantity of food as well as a large amount of weeds, which under present arrangements if not illegally fed, run to seed and stock the neighbourhood with weeds, because the cutting of these banks involves a considerable expense of labour which the neighbouring occupiers or the Highway Board seldom care to expend. Yet there are in most localities, poor families keeping a cow or two, who would gladly feed these banks and tend the cattle well, so that they would be no nuisance to anyone, and an understanding might be come to between neighbours that the lanes might be fed provided the cattle were well tended and the nettles, briars and large weeds be kept down by those who had the benefit of the grass. I know the lanes in my neighbourhood are pretty closely fed by the cows and horses of small occupiers, and though my front gate is seldom closed, and sometimes wide open night and day, I have not seen a stray animal inside for years past.

Samuel Saunders.
Lavington, 5th June 1883.

27th September 1883

Last week, Mr A. Frame of West Lavington put a piece of potato into his mouth at dinner, when a wasp which happened to be upon it stung him in the throat. The sting caused him intense agony, and no little danger.

(It must have been a slow news week!)

21st January 1886

Benjamin Hayward Obituary

Our obituary today records the death of Mr Benjamin Hayward of Easterton, at the advanced age of 95! The last of his generation on the male side, Mr Hayward belonged to one of the oldest and most respected families in Wiltshire. At Beechingstoke, where he will be buried tomorrow, there is no less than forty of the same family, from the time of Queen Elizabeth downward, and in which parish, until the death of the late Mr Joseph Hayward, they had held property for upwards of 200 years.

Mr B. Hayward, the subject of our present notice, had however resided from his boyhood at Lavington and Easterton, which until comparatively recent years, formed part of the parish of Lavington. His father in his day occupied the farm now held by Mr E. Lush at West Lavington (Dial House), and for many years Mr B. Hayward was the tenant of the farm now occupied by Mr Alfred Neate in the same parish, (Pyt House). But this takes us back something like 40 years, for it is quite that time that Mr B. Hayward has lived, retired, at Easterton.

But although retired from business, his life was by no means an inactive one. Possessed of a well stored mind, he took great delight in reading, and as a naturalist, and especially as an ornithologist, he was often quoted as an authority; there was not an English bird with whose habits and peculiarities he was not intimately acquainted; while his clear mind and wonderful recollection of dates made his companionship always interesting and instructive.

Born 9 years before the close of the last century, he had a vivid recollection of all the stirring events which marked the commencement of the present century, and could relate with wonderful memory, the incidents connected with the wars which marked that period, and the intense, almost breathless, anxiety with which the people in those days awaited the news of engagements upon whose issue the fate of England may at times be said to have depended.

His great length of days, extended for something like a quarter of a century beyond the three score years and ten of which the Psalmist speaks, was no doubt due, primarily, to an excellent constitution; but Mr Hayward, without being in any way a teetotaller, was in every sense a moderate man; and a man moreover who took much outdoor exercise. To walk into Devizes from Easterton, and back, was within recent years a mere matter of recreation; and it was only last summer that he was among the spectators at Wombwell's great menagerie, and was able to record his vote at Market Lavington at the late general Election on the 27th November. Indeed up to almost the last moment he was in possession of his faculties. He was a man who will be much missed in his locality; without ostentation, his hand was ever ready to contribute to the charities of the village, and as an evidence of his desire to help those who needed assistance, may be mentioned the munificent subscription of £50 which he gave towards the erection of Easterton National School in 1877. It is remarkable when we come to think of it, that Mr B. Hayward lived one twentieth of the whole time that has elapsed since the birth of our Saviour; and some of his family were even longer lived than himself; his first cousin, Mrs Robbins, having died only a few months ago at the age of 96, while all his brothers, of whom he had five, lived to nearly four score years, and his grandfather to 90.

12th January 1888

Cross Keys Club

This excellent club continues to thrive in West Lavington, and to carry on a most useful work by means of its reading room and coffee tavern. The annual supper of the members and their friends, which usually takes place on New Year's Eve, was held on Monday last. In the unavoidable absence of Mr Kelsey, owing to a cold, Mr Guy Stevenson presided, there being also present: Dr Hitchcock and Messrs J. S. Lush, E. G. Lush, E. H. Green, C. Pomeroy, Nosworthy, A. Axford, Joseph Sainsbury, W. Sainsbury, S. Sainsbury, James Mead, Enos Bartlett, T. Self, J. Glass, J. Cooper, J. Lye, E. Coleman, C. Caple, W. J. Goodman, G. Brown, F. Brown, W. Brown, T. G. Axford, J. King, jun., A. Bamford, A. Rowbottom, J. Chapman, S. Chapman, J. Merrett,

G. Sidford, R. Stevens, T. Woods, J. Crowe, H. Durdin, and W. Baish.

The room was tastefully decorated with evergreens and devices by Miss Carter and Miss Davis, the mottoes including 'God Save the Queen', 'Welcome', 'Loyalty', and 'A Happy New Year'. An excellent supper was provided by Mr and Mrs Collins, and was served in admirable style by the committee. Afterwards a number of toasts and songs were given, a very pleasant evening being passed. The first toast was that of 'The Queen and the Royal Family', which was drunk with the customary loyalty.

The Chairman submitted 'The Army, Navy and Reserve Forces', and spoke of the local Volunteers as belonging to one of the best companies in one of the best Volunteer regiments in England.

Col. Sergt. T. Davis in reply said E. Company had the good fortune to have excellent officers. He was sorry to hear that Lieut. Neate was going to resign, but he hoped they would have Mr Henry Lush in his place [applause]. He considered that the country ought to be much obliged to the Volunteers whose existence had removed the fear of invasion and proved of great use to their country. In conclusion, Col. Sergt. Davis acknowledged the kindness of the employers who let men off to attend drill [hear, hear].

Corpl. Merrett also responded.

The Chairman gave 'Success to the Cross Keys Club, and the health of Mr and Mrs Collins', thanking them for the excellent manner in which they had continued to conduct it and for the capital supper they had laid before the assembly that evening [applause].

Mr Collins acknowledged the toast, and wished all present a prosperous year.

The Chairman proposed 'The Committee', coupled with the names of Mr T. Self and Mr James Mead. Mr Self in reply said he was happy to report that they had a balance in hand, although it was not a very large one. He hoped there would be an increase in the number of members this quarter.

Mr Mead said the committee did their best to keep the Club in working order, and they were very much gratified to see such a large number present. They were deeply indebted to Mr Walter Bouverie, without whose liberality and Mr Collins' obliging and accommodating management, they would be unable to keep going [hear, hear].

Mr J. S. Lush proposed 'the health of Mr Walter Bouverie', to whom they were indebted for his enterprise in starting the Club and Coffee Tavern. He hoped Mr Bouverie would in the future, as in the past, continue to be rewarded by seeing a large number of persons avail themselves of the benefits of the Club. The toast was drunk with musical honours, as also was 'The Health of the Chairman', proposed in complimentary terms by Mr E. H. Green.

Songs were sung in the course of the evening by Mr E. H. Green; the Chairman, with banjo accompaniment; Messrs A. Bamford, T. Smith, A. Rowbottom, J. Mead, E. Coleman, W. Smith, Miss Carter, and others, while recitations were given by Mr J. S. Lush, Mr T. Davis and Miss Davis and Mr J. Crowe.

3rd September 1888

A serious accident happened at West Lavington last night. Mr Carter, manager of the Devizes Water Works in Beckhampton Down, had been with his wife and child to the horticultural show, and was about to get into a waggonette, which was standing at his father's door, and return to Devizes, when a break belonging to Mr Joliffe, driven by a man named Gingell, ran into the vehicle and smashed it almost to atoms. Mrs Carter was already in the waggonette and was so injured by the collision that it has not yet been deemed prudent to remove her; the child escaped unhurt. It was about 9 o'clock when the accident happened, but it was light enough for a careful driver to have avoided the collision. The waggonette belonged to Mr Phipp of the Three Crowns.

16th August 1890

Fire at West Lavington

Between 5 and 6 o'clock on Saturday evening last, a fire broke out in a rick of wheat belonging to Mr Thomas Giddings of Littleton, and situate in a field near the Black Dog Inn, West Lavington. The fire spread rapidly until the rick was nearly destroyed. The total amount of damage done was about £6. The rick was insured in the Royal Farmers' Life Office. A small portion only was saved. A little boy, the son of a farm labourer, is said to have been seen with some matches in the field when the fire was discovered.

Chapter Two
Extreme Weather

6th July 1843

Yesterday afternoon, between 2 and 3 o'clock, two horses which were at plough in a field near Gore Farm were struck by lightning and instantaneously killed. The carter, Mr William Lennard was also struck violently by the electric fluid, and was taken to West Lavington in a state of insensibility, but he is, we are happy to say, likely to recover. The horses were the property of Mr W. Hooper of Cornbury Farm.

3rd July 1851

The Storm of Tuesday

Devizes and various parts of the county were visited with a storm on Tuesday afternoon, which has left behind its devastating traces not readily to be forgotten. In our own neighbourhood especially, its effects have been very disastrous to the crops; whilst in several cases the escape from death by lightning has been most extraordinary.

Besides the mischief caused by the lightning, the torrents of rain and hail that fell have done immense damage. On the farms of Mr W. Sainsbury, Mr Spencer, Mr Hooper and Mr Lawes at Lavington, £1800 it is said, will hardly replace the injury sustained. A correspondent living in that parish says:

"To show the uncertainty of remuneration from the capital employed in agriculture, I send you a few samples of corn taken from different farms at West Lavington. The sample of wheat of Mr Spencer's I valued a few days previous at 8 sacks per acre; it will not now realize more than 6 or 8 bushels at harvest! Mr Hooper's barley, calculated at 5 quarters per acre is nine tenths of it

entirely destroyed! I was at Mr Sainsbury's farm yesterday and a more splendid field of corn and turnips I never wish to behold; about 3 o'clock a tremendous thunder storm commenced and lasted with one continued roar for the space of 2 hours, with vivid flashes of lightning, accompanied with heavy rain and hail. Some of the hail stones were from four to four and a half inches in circumference. Mr Sainsbury's farm, which is nearly the highest point in the county of Wiltshire, was deluged with water from one to three feet deep. On the rain subsiding, it was found to have destroyed several acres of turnips, having turned up the soil to the depth of the plough."

The samples of wheat and barley which our correspondent sent us are so broken in the stalk and otherwise damaged as to render them utterly useless.

The storm however, notwithstanding its violence and extent, seems to have been partial. For instance, in the neighbourhood of Potterne, and even on some of the farms at Lavington adjoining those on which so much damage was done, its effects were scarcely felt; so in other places. It appeared to be at its height between 3 and 4 o'clock, but in about an hour or so afterwards the clouds dispersed, and the evening was as clear and fine as any evening during the week.

4th September 1862

Tremendous Storm and Serious Loss of Property at Lavington

Never within the memory of man, has such a storm been known in this neighbourhood as visited Market and West Lavington and Easterton on Tuesday morning; a storm at once so overwhelming in its consequences as to find a parallel only in the disastrous Shrewton flood, which took place about 23 years ago. The Shrewton flood however, was a flood of water, occasioned by the sudden thaw of an accumulation of snow on the adjacent hills; whereas the storm of Tuesday last was not alone a flood of water, or rain, but a fall of hail, the like of which, we will venture to say, has never before been seen in this country. Indeed, had we not been eyewitnesses of the fact, we could hardly have believed that in less than half an hour hail stones would have stood upon the ground *seven feet deep!* Yet so it was at Lavington on Tuesday morning, and the scene which the country presented will never be forgotten by those who witnessed it.

There had been distant rumblings of thunder and occasional flashes of lightning soon after the day began to dawn, and the sky for miles around wore a heavy, leaden hue; but men nevertheless ventured upon their out-door work, little dreaming of what was about to burst upon them. About half past 5, a roar, as of a roll of musketry, was heard, the lightning and thunder increased, and, as if the bolts of heaven had suddenly been withdrawn, there fell such a deluge of hail and rain as fairly frightened all who beheld it. In less than half an hour the whole line of country, from Easterton on the one side to West Lavington on the other, was completely covered. Not a blade of grass, or corn, or crop of any kind was visible; the whole surface of the earth, was one mass of hailstones; the houses were from two to three feet deep in water – the cellars full up to the very gratings – whilst the streets and roads throughout the whole length from Easterton to West Lavington were converted into a deep, roaring, rushing torrent which carried everything before it. As to the damage done to the crops by the hail, thousands of pounds will not repay it, acres upon acres of barley being left without a single grain on the stalk.

But disastrous as the visitation was, it was extremely partial in its course, and in its extent. Its violence seems to have been limited to about half a mile in breadth and two miles in length, extending diagonally from Gore Cross, along a portion of the hill and valley of the two Lavingtons, as far as Eastcott. Beyond either of these points, we do not hear that any serious damage was sustained; and within half a mile of it, at Candown, for instance, and on Fiddington Hill, so trifling had been the fall, that wheat was being carried within a few hours afterwards.

At Eastcott, the first scene of the disaster presented itself; and a scene indeed it was: every house, with its lower rooms under water, and people looking out from the upper windows of the cottages in momentary expectation of being swept away in the torrent. The water in Mr Jacob Newman's farm was 6 feet deep, and the barrels in his cellar floated about as though they had been in a pond.

By Mr Benjamin Hayward's at Easterton, the water rushed along like a mill stream, carrying with it his wall, Mr Williams's garden wall, the boundary fence at Fiddington House, and in fact everything that came in its way; bricks, timber, and even the road itself, which is gorged up in many places as though it had been lifted up from its foundation by some subterranean force. The greatest wonder is that the cottages were not swept away also; their condition may be imagined, with water in them three feet high, and with no chance of help from anybody, for not a soul could venture from the upper stories without running the risk of being swept away. One man, who had been milking, in his endeavour to drive through the village, after the storm had in some degree subsided, had his milk kettle carried out of his cart, and floated rapidly away along the current; and a piece of timber 10 feet long was carried 40 yards down the middle of the road; and we heard of one cottage, situated in the lower part of Easterton, where the water rose to the ceiling in the lower room, and drowned a cat which happened unfortunately to be without the means of escape; and of another, where a little girl who was left in the room on the ground floor, got upon the table to save herself, and was floated about the room upon it, saving herself eventually by clinging to the sill of the window.

In Fiddington Hollow, near Dr Hitchcock's, the water made a clean breach over the hedge, and in its rush down to the adjoining fields resembled a boiling cataract, which nothing could withstand.

But at Market Lavington, matters were worse even than at Easterton. The only wonder is that the houses in the lower part of the town near the church were left standing. The escape of some of them from destruction is to be attributed to the prompt action of the occupants, who observing that the foundations were about to give way, knocked holes through the walls, and so lessened the weight of water that was rushing against them. The street, from end to end, was like a mighty river, and the roaring of the hail, accompanied with vivid lightning and loud peals of thunder, made the scene truly awful, and filled all hearts with fear. As to the hail; never was such a sight seen before, in this or any other part of the country. In one place, called 'Broadwell', near Mr Fowle's house, it covered the entire space, seven feet deep, and the rush of water from the hill at this point was tremendous. Everything that was in the way went with it, and as an instance of the velocity with which it ran, we may state that 8 loads of flints by the side of the road near Mr Fowle's house were carried entirely away. Mr Fowle was in his yard giving directions to his men, when the storm first burst, and ran for shelter under a skilling, But he had not been there long before the water rose between 3 or 4 feet deep in the yard, and cut off all communication between him and the house; and but for the greatest promptitude, the young livestock that were upon the premises would have been lost. The lower part of Mr Fowle's house was entirely inundated, and such mastery had the storm obtained inside, that Miss Fowle was unable to get to her mother's room for the water that ran through the passages. But the scene at Broadwell, beat everything else; and that the cottages there stood through the storm is perfectly marvellous. In one of them, no less than two feet of mud and sand covered the ground floor, and the water was up so high that the inmates dared not venture downstairs at the peril of their lives. Hundreds of waggon loads of hail lay about at this spot during the day; and in the evening, notwithstanding the extreme heat of the weather, it was 4 feet deep in places. The loss to the crops can hardly at present be estimated. Mr Fowle has acres and acres of corn in which hardly a grain is left in the husk. This is the case with about 26 acres of barley and oats on the hill and near his house; and so with the crops of Mr House (of the Green Dragon Inn) and Mr Farmer. Ten acres of barley belonging to Mr House, estimated to contain at least 4 quarters to the acre, are so skinned that there is not one whole ear left out of ten thousand, and the entire piece will now hardly yield 3 quarters. A piece of oats (of 2 or 3 acres) also belonging to Mr House is reduced to mere husks; and a crop of wheat on the same farm has at least a sack and a half an acre knocked out of it. The effect of the storm upon the allotments is absolutely ruinous. We saw one or two pieces of barley on the land occupied by these smallholders, containing half an acre each, in which it would be difficult to find a quarter of grain left, whilst the turnips, potatoes and other roots were in many cases washed completely out of the ground, and swept away in the torrent, or cut into shreds by the hail.

To recount all the disasters that occurred in Market Lavington would fill a column of our space. Mr Neate's cellars were full of water up to the very gratings, and for hours after the rain had ceased the barrels which they contained might be seen floating about up to the level of the road. A strong brick wall which formed the boundary of the farm yard near the church came down *en masse;* and at Northbrook the flooring of the house occupied by Axford, the dog breaker, was thrust up by the water, and the dogs in the kennels were obliged to swim to save their lives. £20 it is said will not pay the damage done to Axford's premises. In another part of the parish, a carpenter named Rimer, had nearly everything washed out of his house, and narrowly saved the life of his pig, by taking it bodily out of the sty. The disasters among the feathered tribe were innumerable. Ducks were drowned in their favourite element; fowls shared the same fate; and sparrows, thrushes and blackbirds were picked up by hundreds after the storm was over, knocked down by the hail, and buried beneath it. No less than 78 sparrows were picked up dead in the church (which is at present unroofed); and as proof of the destruction which was carried on among these birds, a baker in the place informed us that although hundreds of them had been in the habit of congregating in his yard daily when his chickens were being fed, not one was to be seen during the whole of Tuesday, and hardly a small bird was seen in Market Lavington up to Wednesday morning.

Leaving Market Lavington, we now come to West Lavington; and along the whole line of road from one village to the other, nothing was to be seen but hail, heaped here and there in enormous masses 6 and 7 feet deep. At Cornbury Mill the water rose to a great height; and an acre of barley belonging to the miller (Mr Burbage) was so completely riddled, as to be absolutely worthless. At Russell Mill (occupied by Mr Pearless) the water rose in less than an hour 6 feet at the tail of the mill; and a meadow close by, of Mr Fowle's, was at least six feet under water; whilst in the house attached to the mill there were two feet of water in all the lower rooms.

But the amount of destruction at other places was small in comparison to what took place at Mr Thos Neate's farm at West Lavington. Mr Neate had on the side of the hill 127 acres of barley, one of the finest crops he has ever grown upon the farm, containing at least 5 quarters to the acre (as was proved by some which he had cut and threshed out). The crop was just fit to harvest; in fact 30 acres of it were already laying in swath; and we speak within bounds when we say that the damage which the hail did to this crop will not be covered for less than £800. 70 acres of it are as cleanly threshed, (and washed away), as if the crop had passed through a threshing machine, the ears being stripped completely off, leaving the bare straw denuded of its head. It is estimated that at least 500 quarters are lost out of the 127 acres; and the only satisfaction which Mr Neate has, is that he is fully insured in the Farmer's office; a precaution which he was very nearly foregoing at the commencement of the season, having (as he thought) paid a deal of money uselessly in previous years to secure himself against losses which did not seem likely to occur.

At Mr Lush's house, situated at the foot of the hill leaving West Lavington village for Tilshead, (Dial House), the stream made a clean breach from the back to the front door; inundating all the lower rooms, and setting the tables, chairs and the furniture of the drawing and dining rooms two feet deep in water; whilst the house itself had the appearance of standing in the midst of a lake, the whole of the open space around, presenting one vast sheet of water, from Mr William Sainsbury's to the opposite rising ground. When we paid a visit to the scene on Tuesday, hatches were being fitted to the front and back doors, so as to prevent the passage through the house from being converted into a water course in future, this being the second time within the last few years that Mrs Lush has suffered from an inundation (although the first visitation bore no comparison with that which swept through her house on Tuesday morning).

From this point towards Tilshead the storm pursued its course, but on reaching Gore Cross it seems to have expended its fury, its effect upon the crops there being confined to levelling the barley with the ground (but without threshing it out), and to drenching the root crops (without cutting them to shivers).

For hours afterwards, the country around presented a most extraordinary appearance. Not a sign of vegetation was to be seen in the fields. Instead of standing barley, which had given so rich and golden an appearance to the hillside the evening before, nought met the eye but hail, hail, hail! Burying everything beneath it; whilst the allotments and gardens, the roads, and even the houses, looked as if they had just emerged from a deluge. As to the poor cottagers, their case is indeed pitiable. Many of them who held allotments have lost their entire crop, and the mischief which has been occasioned in their dwellings is sad indeed. Throughout the whole day afterwards they were engaged in wheeling the mud and filth from their rooms, and the dampness and the smell which the inundation left behind it, made them in many cases almost uninhabitable.

Mr Fowle and Mr Neate were, we believe, the only parties insured against damage by hail; and they will, we have no doubt, be liberally dealt with by the office with which their policies are effected. For the poor, who have so greatly suffered, in many instances losing the whole of their crop, on which their entire dependence was staked, we have no doubt a subscription will be set on foot.

12th December 1872

The Hurricane of Sunday Night

Although the hurricane of Sunday night was fortunately unattended with any personal disaster so far as the town of Devizes is concerned, its effects were severely felt in the destruction of property, and that no fatal consequences ensued is mainly to be attributed to the fact of its having occurred in the evening, when few persons were about, and on a day when work ceases.

In all directions we hear of trees being uprooted, walls thrown down, and buildings unroofed, and in one case, two valuable cows were killed.

(There then follows a catalogue of damage in Devizes and surrounding villages.)

Around Lavington the storm left traces of its ravages in every direction. Scores of trees within a narrow circuit of the town were uprooted, whilst ricks and cottages suffered considerably. 5 large elms were blown down in Parsonage Lane, destroying the telegraph wires and putting a stop to communication for a time. But happily injuries to property are the worst we have to record; life and limb have escaped.

Chapter Three
Labourer's Unrest in West Lavington in the 1830s

Following the end of the Napoleonic Wars, life became increasingly difficult for the labouring people in the countryside. Whilst there was a minimum wage in operation for the agricultural worker, this varied according to the size of his family and was related to the price of bread. This meant that wages went up and down with alarming regularity, and the wages paid by the farmer had to be topped up out of the poor rate. There was also a high level of unemployment, as soldiers who had fought for their country were discharged and let loose upon the countryside.

Lord Churchill as lord of the manor was a benevolent landlord. During the 1820s, Lady Churchill sent clothing and blankets for the poor of West Lavington, and in 1824, at the suggestion of his agent here, Mr Henderson, Lord Churchill allocated 36 acres of good land to be divided into allotments of one third or one quarter of an acre each, for the use of the cottagers. This, with their cottage gardens, enabled them to keep a pig, which also supplied manure for their allotment, and they were able to grow their own vegetables.

The villagers were very grateful for this, and it must have made a considerable difference to their lives. They paid a rent of 15 shillings a year for their allotments. In 1830, some further land was added so that, by the end of the year, there were nearly 70 acres of allotments in the hands of 139 families. When Lord Churchill visited West Lavington in December 1830, he was well received by the poor people of the village who thanked him for having granted the allotments.

Mr Henderson described the allotment system he devised in the local press in October 1832 with a letter to the Editor.

11ᵗʰ October 1832

To the Editor of the Devizes Gazette:

Sir,

Having had frequent inquiries made to me relative to the lands let to the Cottagers upon the estate of Lord Churchill at West Lavington, under my superintendence, and called the Fields of Industry, if you can find room in your valuable paper to insert the following statement, perhaps it might be improved upon in other parishes.

I am, Sir, your obedient servant.
C. R. Henderson, Agent.
West Lavington, 9ᵗʰ October 1832.

In 1824, upon 36 acres of good land falling into hand close by the village, I recommended to Lord Churchill to divide it amongst the Cottagers, to be cultivated by the spade. The names of the heads of families were taken, the land measured into lots, the number of each lot cut upon the ground, and the same number wrote upon tickets. The names of the Cottagers were then called over, who each drew a ticket and took possession of the lot whose number corresponded with that on the ticket.

The land being so laid out, each lot was provided with an opening to the common roads in the laying out, which prevented any person from trespassing upon the land of another. The tenants being thankful, and their ground well cultivated, about 30 acres more of good land coming into hand near the village in 1830, the same was allotted and divided as before, to supply those who were not provided for in 1824.

Lord Churchill pays all rates and outgoings, the tenants having nothing to pay but the fixed rent. The industry of the cottagers and the advantages of spade husbandry, enable them to obtain full one fourth more without fallow, than land of the same quality adjoining, cultivated in the common way by the plough.

From experience I have no doubt wherever local circumstances are favourable to adopting the plan of letting small lots of ground to the cottagers, that it will prove a great advantage in creating industrious habits, good morals, and a little independence, amongst that useful body, the agricultural labourers of this country. But in this case several things must be attended to; the land must be of a good quality situate near the village or town, that little time may be lost in going and coming; it must be rented from the principal landlord, and the rents paid to him or his agent, for this system seldom works well if the land is rented under the Overseers of the parish; and the tenants themselves should be of industrious habits.

I consider no loss is sustained between the cultivation of the cottager's lot and attention to their master's employ, a great part of their labour being done by the women and children. At day break here in West Lavington may be seen those fields of industry full of labourers, from the age of 5 years up to 70, all at work until 6 o' clock, and the same from 6 in the evening until dark, and some at work by moonlight.

The largest families have one third of an acre, and the others one quarter of an acre, and this with their cottage gardens enables them to keep a pig, which makes manure for their land; they pay their rent in October, on a day which I appoint, giving them sufficient notice, and they are all punctual to the time.

The whole land let upon this plan on Lord Churchill's estate is upwards of 66 acres, divided among 139 families. I don't confine them to any particular crop; they are at liberty to plant it with what they please, provided it is done by spade in a neat husbandlike manner. I have a printed paper as to their conduct towards each other, etc, and every tenant has a copy of the same. It is understood that in case of misconduct or bad husbandry, the land is to be taken away, without notice, as soon as the crops are cleared, and given to another person more deserving. With a few exceptions the principal part of the tenants are agricultural labourers. I have carried on the same plan in Oxfordshire, and it prospers in every respect.

****

So at the beginning of the 1830s, there were grounds for optimism in the village. The villagers, in return for this favourable treatment, were punctual in the payment of their rents and had not participated in the recent Swing Riots.

The Swing Riots had started in Kent in the summer of 1830. The agricultural labourers demanded a minimum wage, the end of unemployment, and reductions in rents. The riots spread throughout the South East of England and as far as Wiltshire, but clearly at this stage there was not a problem in West Lavington.

However by the spring of 1831, the agricultural labourers of West Lavington made the National press. The following is an article in the London Standard:

4th June 1831

West Lavington: Strike Among the Agricultural Labourers

About 50 able-bodied labourers in the employ of 4 farmers of the parish of West Lavington, refused to work on Monday last, in consequence of their employers, on the previous Saturday, reducing their wages from 9 to 8 shillings per week. The men came in a body to Devizes on Monday morning, for the purpose of appealing to the Magistrates; but unfortunately every Magistrate of the division, with the exception of one, was from home.

On Tuesday, the men were again in Devizes, at an early hour of the morning; at noon the Magistrates, Mr Scott and Mr Ludlow, who had been sitting at the Petty Sessions sent for one of them, and accordingly a stout brawny man, who conducted himself with the greatest propriety, soon made his appearance.

He stated that his master, and other farmers in West Lavington, had for some time past paid their labourers 9 shillings a week. But that on Saturday last, without any previous notice, they refused to give more than 8 shillings for that week's work, which they said was to be the future rate of wages. The labourers, in consequence, felt dissatisfied and refused to work.

For himself he said that he had a wife and 7 children, and that a reduction of 1 shilling out of 9 was a hardship not easily to be borne. He spoke of the general kindness of his master, Mr Sainsbury, and also of the Overseer; but he would leave it to any labourer with whom, or to any master for whom he had ever worked, whether he did not labour hard, and fare harder.

"From the beginning to the end of the week," he said, "Even from the beginning to the end of the year, I never take into the field more than a bit of dry bread for my dinner, and at this moment there is not the smallest quantity of victuals in my house."

Notwithstanding he and his fellow labourers were greatly dissatisfied, he said they wished to act peaceably. They would be content with 9 shillings a week, and be trusted that, through the Magistrates, the farmers would be induced to continue that rate of wages. Nothing could excel the conduct of this man, and the Magistrates themselves appeared to enter into his feelings, and to think that 9 shillings a week was not a farthing too much for the labour of an able-bodied man. They however justly observed that they had no power whatever to interfere. They recommended the men to return to their work, and take task-work instead of day-work. This, however the man with 7 children said, would not be better, for all descriptions of work were lowered. A gentleman present observed that the farmers complained of, were obliged to lower the wages of their labourers in consequence of their landlords advancing their rents.

The Magistrates could scarcely credit the assertion that any landlord would, in times like the present, advance his rents. They were perfectly astounded when it was positively stated that Lord Churchill, at his recent audit, advanced the rents of his tenants at West Lavington 10 per cent. It was further stated that the produce of the farms of these tenants, during the last year, did not by some considerable sum, pay the rental; and that they expected a reduction instead of an advance.

The man with 7 children observed that Lord Churchill had taken off 10 per cent at a former audit, in order that the tenants might raise the wages of the labourers from seven shillings to ten shillings a week, but as the tenants had not done this, his lordship again laid on the 10 per cent. We have been informed however, by a very respectable farmer, that the advance the tenants did make in the wages of their labourers far more than counterbalanced the reduction his lordship made in his rentals; and that it is impossible the farmers can, for any length of time, pay even 8 shillings a week, without some considerable abatement in rent.

We are happy to state that the labourers yesterday morning quietly returned to their work.

****

This peaceful strike by the agricultural labourers of West Lavington took place nearly 3 years before the Tolpuddle Martyrs were convicted for their Union activities. It isn't known whether there was any improvement for the labourers after their strike, but if there was it was relatively short lived. By 1834, when a new system of Poor Laws came into force, there was much dissatisfaction within the rural community. And in 1850, a similar situation arose when the labourer's wages were only 6 shillings a week. Further strike action was threatened as follows:

21st February 1850

Threatened Disturbance Among the Labourers at West Lavington

Much excitement has prevailed in the neighbourhood of West Lavington during the last 3 days, owing to a strike and threatened disturbances among the labourers, in consequence of a notice which was given on Saturday night by most of the principal farmers of an intention to reduce the rate of wages from 7s to 6s a week, the sum paid for some time past in most of the adjoining parishes. Some intimation of this intention had, it appears, been given to the men a fortnight ago, and in the hope of averting it, a large number of them went on Monday week to Mr Kelsey, the steward of Lord Churchill, who is the owner of the principal farms in the parish, and begged him to intercede in their behalf.

This Mr Kelsey, we are informed, promised he would do, cautioning them at the same time not to leave the week's work which they had begun, and thus render themselves liable to a conviction. Upon this the men quietly returned to their usual occupations, but finding that their masters were firm in the determination they had come to, early on Monday morning about 150 of the malcontents met in a body in front of the house of Mr Spencer, a considerable farmer in the parish, and stopped man, horse and implement from proceeding to work by that road. Having thus persuaded or forced as many as possible to join them, they proceeded to the different farms, stopped all operations that were going on, took the horses from the plough, and turned them loose in the field, opened the sheep folds etc, and prevented men women and children from pursuing their work. At Cornbury Farm, Mr William

Hooper, the occupier happened to be in his field when the mob arrived. They demanded that the plough should stop and the ploughman and others who were present join the force, and in spite of all remonstrations from Mr Hooper, and contrary to the men's wish, they were forced off. The same course was carried on throughout the day upon all the different farms in the parish.

No serious breach of the peace however took place, and on Tuesday morning, a considerable portion of those who had reluctantly left their employment on the preceding day, returned to work; but towards night, in consequence it is said of a rumour that warrants had been issued for the apprehension of the ringleaders in the revolt, and that an attempt was to be made that evening to take them into custody, upwards of 100 men formed themselves into a band, and paraded the streets, armed with fold staves.

Upon this, an express was immediately sent to Captain Meredith, the Chief Constable, who had previously visited the parish, but withdrawn the greater portion of his men upon finding a disposition on the part of the labourers to return to work and conduct themselves properly.

At about midnight the Captain, with Superintendent Wolfe and a strong body of police arrived and remained on guard during the night and the following morning. Previous to their arrival however, the labourers had separated and repaired to their homes without having molested anyone, or given any cause for alarm beyond their formidable appearance; and we are happy to hear that no further evidence of a disturbance has since been exhibited.

The publicans in the parish, either from order, or from sound discretion, refused to sell beer on the day of the men first striking work, and thus prevented much noise and strife which might otherwise have ensued.

From what we have been able to glean, the question of wages does not appear to be the only one issue in this case, and we are rejoiced to add that no symptom of personal hostility has been evinced towards the farmers of the parish, who are generally speaking honourable men, men who are well disposed towards their labourers, and who are desirous of paying them to the utmost ability, as is shown from the fact of their having continued up to the present time, to pay 1 shilling a week more than has been paid for months past in many other parishes. Allotment rents and house rents seem to be mixed up in the detail of griēvances of which the men complain, but as the whole case will in all probability form the subject of an early legal investigation, when facts will be elicited and a full statement supplied upon evidence, we should be sorry, with our present imperfect knowledge of all the circumstances attending the revolt, to say anything which might prejudice the course of justice or compromise the representations which have been made to us either on one side or the other.

This morning, one of the men (named Kite) who had taken an active part in forcing the labourers upon the different farms to leave their work, was brought up in custody before the Magistrates in Devizes and remanded for further examination. Scarcely had he been taken from the police-office and conveyed to prison, when a large body of labourers, having heard of his capture, arrived in town, armed with sticks, for the purpose of rescuing him. Their arrival however was too late to enable them to make their contemplated attempt, but the determined language which escaped from them upon finding themselves foiled, lead us to fear that unless due precautions are taken, some violence may be committed on their return home.

28th February 1850

In the previous gazette we gave some particulars respecting the strike and threatened disturbance amongst the labourers at West Lavington, in consequence of notice of an intended reduction of wages. We have now the satisfaction of stating that these mistaken men have all returned quietly to their work, and that one of the ringleaders, a man named Kite, who had been apprehended and brought before the Magistrates on Thursday last when he was remanded, was again brought up on Monday and discharged. This man was really deserving of punishment as he had taken a leading part in preventing other labourers, particularly those on Cornbury Farm, from following their trade, but he was leniently treated in consequence of the humanity of Mr Hooper, the occupier of that farm who had to his credit declined to press the charge. The culprit however received a severe reprimand from Admiral Bouverie who told him truly that he was indebted to the forbearance of Mr Hooper, for, had he been prosecuted and convicted he would have been sentenced to hard labour for two years. He was, added the Magistrate, at liberty to work or not as he pleased, but he had no right to coerce others.

6 shillings a week are certainly small wages, and the labourers are to be commiserated. But they ought to remember that their condition cannot be bettered by strikes, combinations and acts of violence. All such attempts have never failed to recoil on the heads of those who made them, and ample experience has shown that every such movement has only aggravated tenfold the distress of those who have joined it.

The labourers, besides, cannot fail to be aware that the farmers can scarcely afford in these disastrous times to give them the wages they actually receive. The farmers and labourers are joint sufferers from the fatal system, the work of the nefarious coalition of Whigs and Radicals with the renegade chief of the conservative party, which is plunging the whole country into ruin. The labourers, instead of breaking out into violence against those who are really their stay and their support, ought to make common cause with them in demanding the justice to which both classes are equally entitled from the legislature of their country.

We are also reminded that in many cases of apparently peculiar destitution, all the particulars are seldom known to those not immediately interested. In speaking of the wages of a labouring man with a family, when the rate of his wages is held up to notice, the earnings of his family should in fairness be mentioned also. Up to the period of reducing wages, the man Kite received in this mode 16 shillings and ninepence a week. Good however may result from a movement which every lover of peace and every real friend of the agricultural labourer must deeply regret. The farm servant will henceforth cease to indulge an unreasonable expectation, that the price of *his* labour will not, for a long time, and in ascertainable proportion, fluctuate with the price of corn; and it will also be evident that the wages of labour can be under no other control, nor affected by any other decision, than that of the party by whom those wages are paid. If, as we hinted last week, the price of allotment land, and high cottage rents, under the diminished price of produce, have entered into their account of grievances, they will now fully understand that their masters are fellow sufferers in the existing agricultural depression, however produced, and by whatever means to be relieved or palliated. One thing we are glad to see is unquestionable, with a few marked exceptions, a strong bond seems still to unite the agricultural labourers of West Lavington to their employers, and after misunderstandings and misapprehensions were partially explained and misrepresentations fairly refuted, they were willing to be convinced, and readily acted upon their convictions.

In this case we trust that a forgiving spirit will remove all unpleasant recollections of past transactions, and that if there be just causes of complaint which admit a remedy, a remedy will be speedily applied. The interests of proprietor, occupier and cultivators of the soil should alike be studied, not merely in every legislative enactment connected with this particular branch of national wealth, but in those specific contracts and mutual arrangements which are, or ought to be, mutual advantages.

28th February 1850

Magistrates Office, Devizes

A man named Kite, who was remanded from Thursday last, on a charge of preventing the labourers on Mr Hooper's farm at West Lavington from pursuing their work, was brought up on Monday morning, and at the earnest intercession of Mr Hooper, liberated. Previous to his discharge, however, Admiral Bouverie endeavoured to impress upon him the very serious character of his offence, observing that if Mr Hooper had prosecuted him, and he had been found guilty, he would be liable to 2 years' imprisonment with hard labour. He was at liberty to work or not as he pleased, but he could not coerce others with impunity. He and a number of other labourers had been engaged in a very dangerous and illegal proceeding. They had not only neglected their own occupations, but had prevented others, who were peaceably disposed, from pursuing theirs. And on Thursday morning, many of his companions had had the temerity to arm themselves with sticks, and to walk into the town, for the purpose of obstructing the course of justice. However they listened patiently to the good advice which was then given to them, and they had since returned quietly to their work. From these circumstances, and from the good character which the prisoner had previously borne, he was disposed to listen to Mr Hooper, but in discharging him, he would earnestly caution him as to his future conduct.

11th April 1850

Chief Constable's Report

I have the honour to report that the present effective strength of the Constabulary Force is 9 superintendents, 10 inspectors, 24 sergeants, 135 first class constables, 19 second class constables, 197 now effective. One sergeant has a broken leg, one first class constable is sick, total 199.

This force is stationed in the different police divisions of the county agreeable to the monthly returns which have been transmitted to the Clerk to the Peace for the information of the Court.

I submit a return of the number of persons who have come under cognizance of the police since the last Quarter Sessions, with the result of the proceedings held upon them. Also a return of the offences which have been reported to the police, and the offenders not apprehended.

I have much satisfaction in stating that these returns show a great decrease in the numbers committed for trial, as compared with the corresponding quarter last year, and that crime generally has much decreased in this county.

There has recently been a little excitement at West Lavington and Figheldean with the agricultural labourers, in consequence of their employers reducing their wages, but no serious consequences ensued, and the men resumed their work in an orderly and regular manner.

It having been reported to me that two political meetings were to be held in Swindon on 6th February last, I ordered a strong body of police to assemble, and who remained under my own superintendence until the collective mass of the people had dispersed, and although much excitement prevailed, not any breach of the peace occurred.

A fire broke out at 7.50 pm on the 10th March last at Bayntun Down Farm, in the occupation of Mr James Grant, which is supposed to be an act of an incendiary, but notwithstanding every possible exertion has been used by the police to trace the origin of this fire, not any satisfactory clue has yet been obtained.

Samuel Meredith
Chief Constable

It looks as if the difficulties of the preceding decades were largely a thing of the past by the 1860s.

31st March 1864

West Lavington: The occupants of allotments in this parish held a meeting in the schoolroom on Saturday the 26th inst., at 7 o'clock in the evening, to present a token of their esteem to the Right Hon. Lord Churchill, lord of the manor, and at the same time to show some mark of their gratitude to his lordship's able steward, E. E. P. Kelsey Esq.

The Rev Dr Wilkinson, who had, as he stated, somewhat reluctantly consented to take the chair, then put before the meeting the object of their coming together, and left the first proposal to Mr Daniel Oatley, who, seconded by Mr T. Sawyer, proposed that an address should be presented to Lord Churchill, from the allottees of his manor. Mr Oatley adverted at considerable length to the highly prosperous state of the parish, both in a moral and intellectual point of view, which he attributed to several causes, viz., to the good feeling which existed between all the parishioners, to the allotment system, and to the parish night-school.

The next motion was proposed by Mr Smith and seconded by Mr John Staples, that an address should also be presented to Mr Kelsey. That gentleman then in very touching language thanked the meeting most cordially in behalf of Lord Churchill and himself. But something more substantial than these addresses was presented by the meeting to their respected lord of the manor and his steward. To his lordship was transmitted through Mr Kelsey's hands a Bible, bound in the richest purple morocco, magnificently stamped with ornaments in relief, and bearing a silver plate with an inscription expressive of their highest esteem; while to Mr Kelsey was presented an elaborately chased gold ring set with a precious stone, with the worthy gentleman's crest.

Chapter Four
The Poor laws

When a man was out of work, he was put to work on the roads, and paid wages for his work from the poor rates. The wages were deliberately set at a lower rate than the wages paid to someone who was in regular employment. In addition there were allowances for dependents.

In 1834, it was these road labourers who complained about the hardships that prevailed.

1st May 1834

Devizes Petty Sessions, 29th April 1834
The West Lavington Road Labourers

Several labourers from the parish of West Lavington attended before the Magistrates to make a complaint against the Overseer, for reducing their allowance money. They were introduced one by one.

The first labourer stated that he had a wife and four children, neither of whom could earn a farthing; that he himself was put to work on the roads, for which he had formerly been paid 7 shillings a week, with an allowance of 2 shillings from the parish; but from this small sum to maintain so large a family, and out of which he had to pay ninepence a week rent, 1 shilling was last week deducted.

The Overseer stated that the complainant was one of a number who worked on the roads; that the regular hours of work was from 6 in the morning to 6 in the evening, with an allowance of 2 hours during the day for refreshment. But the men last week positively refused to work after 5 in the evening, and that the complainant in particular intimidated others, and threatened to throw them into the pond if they worked longer. He therefore deducted 1 shilling for the time lost.

The labourer said that he worked the regular number of hours, but instead of taking 2 hours during the day, he took only 1, and left off an hour earlier in the evening.

The Magistrates told him he must conform to the rule prescribed by the parish, or the Overseer would be justified in deducting his wages.

The second labourer stated that he had a wife and 4 children and that his wife expected shortly to be confined with a fifth. For the last fortnight he received only 14s 6d, being 7s 3d a week. The Overseer observed that he also refused to work regular hours, and in consequence a deduction was made from his wages. The labourer replied that he went to work with the other labourers of the parish at 6 in the morning, and returned with them at 5 in the evening, and he would leave it to anybody, whether those were not enough hours enough for so small a sum. He had, he said, a sick wife and not a bit of victuals in the house, nor had he any ground to till potatoes.

The Magistrates told him that he was at liberty to leave the roads the moment he could procure better employment; that he was merely put there to prevent him from starving whilst out of regular work, but during his continuance there, he must work at the hours laid down. At the same time he kindly advised him to apply to Mr Henderson, who might grant him a small plot of ground for potatoes.

A third labourer made a similar complaint, but this man, it was proved, after receiving his wages and allowance on Saturday night, went to the beer-house, accompanied by his wife, where they remained drinking and singing like nightingales until 11 o'clock. The Magistrates held that an Overseer would be justified in withholding assistance for a time, from anyone caught in a beer-house. The parish pay was a charity, not to be squandered in drunkenness.

A fourth labourer made his complaint with no better success.

29th May 1834

A labourer from Lavington stated that he had been at work on the roads at 8d a day, but because his wife had also been at work, and had earned 7d a day, the Overseer contended that this 7d ought to be deducted from his 8d thus wanting him to work from 6 in the morning till 6 at night for 1d a day, in order that their united earnings might be reduced to 4s a week. The Overseer said the man had neglected his work on the road, and that when told his wages should be stopped for such neglect, he threatened to slat his (the Overseer's) skull. The Magistrates said the Overseer was justified in deducting for loss of time; but certainly he ought not to deduct the wife's from the husband's earnings when both were employed.

26th June 1834

There has recently been great dissatisfaction among the labourers at West Lavington. Men with large families have preferred being kept on the roads, having the allowance for their wives and unemployed children made up, according to the scale, amounting in some cases to 10s or 11s a week. Besides this, those labourers have been in the habit of receiving the earnings of one, two or three of their elder children, to the tune of 7 shillings a week; altogether 16s or 17s a week, being considerably more than the Magistrate's scale.

In making up the allowance, the pay masters have at length determined to take into consideration the earnings of the whole family, so that in several instances reductions have been made. The parties who considered themselves aggrieved therefore, made their complaint to the Magistrates on Tuesday; but every case was decided in favour of the Overseer, who was highly complimented by the Magistrates, not only for the manner in which he conducted the affairs at Lavington, but also for his excellent management during the time he was Overseer of the turbulent parish of Urchfont.

The men on the roads have also an idea that they must have their pay whether they work or play, and on one of them being found fault with for idling, he very coolly replied, "My money is sure. I am only anxiously looking for the sun to go merrily round towards the west.". Another labourer, on being told that his wages would be stopped, actually threatened to murder the Overseer if he dared do it. The fellow was bound over to keep the peace.

****

It wasn't just the road labourers who had problems with the new application of the Poor Laws. The Overseers of the Poor were under pressure to reduce the charges on the parish from the poor rate, and this resulted in some very hard decisions.

20th November 1834

A grey haired old man from the parish of West Lavington was summoned to show cause why he refused to maintain one of his grand-children. The old man stated that he had bred up 11 children, without the slightest aid from the parish, and he should be very sorry, in his old years, to be compelled to ask that aid for himself. This would be the case, he said, if he was called upon to maintain one of his grandchildren, as the little property he had left afforded a bare subsistence for himself and his aged wife. It was utterly impossible that he could spare any of it.

The Overseer of West Lavington said that he was instructed to state to the Magistrates that, from the property the old man was in possession of, he could very well afford to give the assistance required of him.

The Magistrates enquired the nature of the property and they were told that it consisted of 7 acres of arable land, which was worth about 50 shillings an acre. Upon this, the Magistrates observed that if this were all, the old man could have little or nothing to spare, especially after poor rates and tithes were deducted. They therefore submitted to the Overseer whether the course he was pursuing was not likely to drive the old man himself to the parish, and strongly advised him not to press the case, or at any rate to consult with the vestry before he did so.

The Overseer said it was far from his wish to oppress the old man, and he would readily follow the advice of the Magistrates.

A pretty looking young woman from West Lavington, who had the misfortune to have an illegitimate child about 3 years ago, complained that the parish had recently stopped the pay for maintenance of this child. The Overseer replied that the parish had very good cause for so doing. The complainant had been married about a fortnight since, and coming under the provisions of the new Poor Law Act, the burden was transferred from the parish to her husband.

"Then that is a complete bar to your demand," said the Magistrate to the woman. "Your husband has taken you for better, for worse; and he is certainly liable to all your encumbrances."

The husband, who was present, appeared thunderstruck at the observations of the Magistrates, and it was a minute or two before he recovered himself. His wife, afraid to encounter him, turned aside her head, and exhibited a sad spectacle of shame and dejection.

Upwards of a dozen fine young men, labourers from West Lavington, appeared before the Magistrates, to make a complaint regarding the rate of wages and allowance. Our readers may recollect that among the recent suggestions of the Commissioners under the new Poor Law Act to the Overseers of the parishes, they recommended "that the allowance to be given to the pauper in return for work provided for him by the parish, whether the same be day work or task work, should be considerably less than the ordinary wages paid for similar work to an independent labourer."

Lyn Dyson

The parish officers of West Lavington are about to act upon this suggestion; and have also given notice that in future the allowance for each child of a pauper will be reduced from 1s to 10d a week; but that the allowance of 1 shilling a week will be continued for each child of a farmer's labourer.

This intended regulation has given much dissatisfaction to those who work on the roads; and as we have stated above, upwards of a dozen of them made their appearance before the Magistrates on Tuesday. They stated that they had gone from parish to parish in search of work, but could find none; and that it was very hard they should be punished for their misfortune. One of them observed that he had a wife who was subject to fits, and 3 children, for the maintenance of all of whom, he was in future to be allowed 6 shillings and sixpence a week only! Out of this house rent was to be paid, which amounted to £3.10s a year, and very nearly a shilling a week in fuel.

Major Olivier observed that probably when the Poor Law Commissioners offered the suggestion alluded to, they did not contemplate the present very low rate of wages of 7 shillings a week. However Mr Scott, the Overseer said in answer that he considered, from the great reduction in the price of wheat, 7 shillings a week now was at least equal to 9 shillings a week some time ago.

The men were at length told that it would be time enough to complain, when the reduction took place. The Magistrates also told them that in future, before they made a complaint, they must demand relief of two Overseers of the parish, and in case relief should be refused, they must make a complaint on oath of such refusal before a Magistrate, who will summon the Overseers to answer the complaint before the Justices at Petty Sessions.

Mr Phipps advised them not again to come in a body; for if by that means they sought to intimidate the Magistrates, they deceived themselves.

Some allusion having been made to the price of bread, Mr Simon Hitchcock, a highly respectable farmer of Allcannings observed that he could obtain no more than 21s a sack for the best of this year's wheat; and that at that rate, the gallon loaf ought to be sold for 10d.

4th December 1834

A cripple from the parish of West Lavington complained that the Overseer had last week deducted 6d from his usual allowance. The Overseer stated that the complainant had been allowed 2s 6d a week, but being in the habit of getting tipsy, he was told a fortnight since that if was ever seen in that state again, his allowance would be reduced.

On Thursday last he was found beastly drunk, rolling in the mud, in consequence of which the vestry ordered that 6d should be taken off from his weekly pay. The Magistrates said the parish acted perfectly right; if paid in money, his allowance should be reduced to the lowest scale; but the better way would be to pay such persons in bread. The man said that he went to see his sister who was going to London and that they had a little beer together before she started, which got the better of him.

16th April 1835

There were several complainants from West Lavington. In this parish the first act of the new Overseer appears to have been to reduce the pay of the paupers on the average 3d a head.

A man, apparently about 25 years of age, and a cripple who has been in the Hospital and is incapacitated for work, complained that he had only 13d a week. The Magistrates thought that in cases of affliction like this, it was very wrong to calculate, with mathematical precision, what was barely necessary to keep persons from actual starvation. The deputy Overseer, a very humane man, and who has been frequently complimented by the Bench, said he would immediately bring the case before the Vestry. In another case from this parish, the Magistrates said they did not think there was sufficient allowed the paupers.

1st October 1835

A poor woman from the parish of West Lavington stated that she had 5 children unable to maintain themselves; that her husband was in constant employ, but that he received only 6s a week, which was not enough for their support. The parish refused to allow them a single farthing, which she could not account for, except that some time since, a child of her sister, who resides in London, was taken very ill, and thinking it might be better in the country, it came to live with her, whilst one of her children went to live with her sister:

"You say that you have four children at home besides the child of your sister, and that your husband only receives 6 shillings a week?" asked the Magistrate.

The woman answered in the affirmative.

"Then that is not sufficient," said the Magistrate.

Mr Sainsbury, the Overseer, said that what the woman had stated was perfectly correct; she had but 6 shillings a week. She had merely omitted to state that her husband had 40lng of ground.

"For which he pays 15 shillings a year," the woman pointed out.

Mr Estcourt, the Magistrate, said: "They can't support themselves upon 6 shillings a week. They can't possibly live upon it!"

"That is my opinion," confirmed the Overseer. "I don't think they can, and I have always been of that opinion; but my brother Overseer, Mr John Hooper, thinks otherwise, and he refused to allow anything from the poor's rate.

"An order must be made for relief," said Mr Estcourt. "Besides, I think it would be extremely wrong to take advantage of the mere exchange of children, under such circumstances. If she had not her sister's child, she would have her own to provide for."

Mr Locke suggested that the mere recommendation of the Magistrates might have the same effect as an order; and a written recommendation was finally agreed to.

At the same time that the Overseers of the Poor were receiving criticism from the poor, they were also having to deal with criticism from those who paid the poor rate. The following case was reported in the Devizes and Wiltshire Gazette on 29th May 1834:

A parishioner of West Lavington had been summoned for the non-payment of the poor rate, but on the morning of Tuesday, the day on which the Petty Sessions were held, he called upon the Overseer and desired him to give a receipt for the rate, and he would pay the assessment. The Overseer wrote the receipt, but the very moment it was finished the fellow snatched it up, and putting the bare amount of the rate upon the table, told the Overseer he might go to Jericho for the costs.

The Overseer remonstrated with him, but he held the receipt up in triumph, and set him at defiance. The Overseer now asked the Magistrates what course must be pursued to compel the man to pay the costs of the summons and the service. The Magistrates said they had no power to interfere; they could only advise him to be very cautious in his future dealings with such sharp-practised gentry; and this advice, we have no doubt, the Overseer will strictly follow.

Lord Churchill, was well aware of the difficulties within the manor of West Lavington, and tried to mitigate them again by reducing the rent his tenants paid to him by ten per cent in late 1835. This was no doubt done so that the tenants could pay their labourers appropriately in the very difficult times.

Chapter Five
Abolition of the Turnpikes

The first Act of Parliament, for the purpose of erecting turnpikes in the area, was passed in 1756. It was estimated that the tolls from the turnpikes had raised about £11,000 over and above the remunerations of the toll-keepers and other expenses, but a mere trifle had been laid out in repairing the roads.

In 1824, Amram Saunders set up a subscription to raise funds to buy the lease of the local turnpikes. They raised £2051 and the purchase of the lease was accomplished.

In December 1824, the following article appeared in the Devizes and Wiltshire Gazette:

For the last 3 months, the spirited inhabitants of Market Lavington and its neighbourhood have been exerting themselves to raise a subscription for the purpose of discharging the debt due to the mortgagees of the Market Lavington Turnpike Roads, and throwing open 9 turnpike gates in the District. We are happy to learn that their object will be readily accomplished. The amount of the debt is £1879, and the sum already subscribed, added to that which it is calculated the sale of the toll gates and houses will produce, will nearly make up the required amount.

There is certainly very great credit due to the gentlemen who first took the measure in hand, by whose perseverance and liberality it has been brought to this happy termination, and but for whom, within a few weeks, another Act of Parliament would be obtained for the purpose of continuing the Trust, and several hundreds more added to the existing debt. The gates and houses, we are informed, will shortly be brought to the hammer by Mr Crocket of that town. Mr Bennett, one of our County Members, has expressed his willingness to contribute to the subscription.

****

In January 1825, plans were announced for the removal of the toll gates on 8th February. The announcement was made in the Devizes and Wiltshire gazette as follows:

We understand that the money which has been raised by voluntary contribution, together with what has been, or will be, derived from the sale of the Turnpike Houses and gates etc, will be sufficient to discharge the whole of the debt on the Market Lavington District of roads. Consequently on Tuesday the 8th February next, nearly, if not all, the Turnpike Gates on that district will be taken down. That day is therefore to be highly celebrated by the inhabitants of Market Lavington and its vicinity. It is intended to have a dinner at the Green Dragon Inn, for as many as can be accommodated; dinners are also to be provided at the other inns for different parties. In the evening there is to be a large bonfire on Lavington Hill, which being a very high spot, will be conspicuous at a great distance.

We believe this is the first instance in the Kingdom of a whole district being cleared of Turnpike Gates by voluntary contribution. It does considerable credit to the neighbourhood, and a list of the contributors, with a full statement of the account is, we understand, shortly to be given to the public. The number of gates on this district are 12, standing at nine different places.

****

In February 1825, a party of men from Market Lavington and Littleton Panell, led by Amram Saunders, raided the toll gates, took them off their hinges and paraded with them through the streets before carrying them up White Street and onto the Plain for a bonfire.

A public dinner was held at the Green Dragon Inn, Market Lavington on 8th February 1825 to celebrate the abolition of the turnpike gates on the Lavington roads. Although nearly 100 people applied for tickets, there was only enough room for 50 people.

The ladies of the village decorated the room with flowers and laurels, and Mr Philpot, the landlord, provided an excellent dinner.

The Hon. Captain Bouverie officiated as President, and there was a band stationed in the yard, occasionally playing some excellent tunes. Among those present were Mr Watson Taylor, Mr Walter Long of Baynton House, the Rev Mr Edmondstone, the Rev Mr Williams, Mr Tinker, Mr Gent of Devizes, Mr Tylce, Mr Saunders, Mr Fowle, Mr Moule of Melksham, and Mr Wayte.

The Hon. Chairman congratulated the company on being assembled to commemorate their success in relieving themselves from the hardship of being subject to taxation without deriving any corresponding benefit therefrom; the hardship of paying tolls, the product of which was not applicable to the repairs of the roads. He then gave an historical review of the turnpike gates in that district from the commencement of their erection to the present time.

The evening was spent in toasting each and every person who had subscribed to the event. A bonfire was lit on Market Lavington Hill, and there were fireworks, and much noise from the firing of cannon.

Chapter Six
Inquest Reports

17th March 1842

An inquest was held by George Sylvester Esq. at West Lavington on the 14th inst. on view of the body of Ann Topp aged 29 years, who was proceeding towards her own residence with her 2 children, the youngest only 4 months old, when a neighbour heard the cries from the children. On going to them, she found the deceased had fallen to the ground, with one foot on the stomach of the infant, and had immediately expired, supposed from an apoplectic seizure. Verdict: died by the visitation of God.

(Ann was the wife of agricultural labourer, Daniel Top. Following her death, Daniel and his son John, who was only three years old, went to live with Daniel's mother and stepfather. Daniel and Ann's daughter, Ann, who was only a year old when her mother died, went to live with her maternal grandparents.)

August 1842

Melancholy Accident

Mr Whitmarsh held an inquest at Potterne on Friday last on the body of Jonathan Sainsbury, a market gardener of West Lavington. The deceased it appears was returning home from Devizes market between 7 and 8 o'clock on the preceding evening with his cart loaded with deal planks, and on going down the hill near Potterne church, the horse, overpowered by the weight of the load, started off at full speed into the village. Sainsbury however soon overtook it, and immediately ran towards the animal, to prevent its progress, but while endeavouring to hold it by the head, he was struck by the timber of his cart, and dragged several yards, when he fell and the wheel passing over his body killed him on the spot. The deceased was 44 years of age, was a man of good character, and we regret to add he left a widow and 9 children, the youngest of whom is only a fortnight old. The jury returned a verdict of accidental death.

(Jonathan's wife was Hannah Chapman, who was twice committed to the House of Correction in Devizes for lewd behaviour in 1826 and 1829, each time for a whole year. It is difficult to imagine what she could have done to deserve such a penalty, but clearly she must have offended a lot of people to be put away for so long!

Hannah was born in 1801, and was the grand-daughter of David Saunders, the pious shepherd. It may be that she was brought up very strictly and felt the need to rebel. She did have a daughter, Anne, born in 1821, another daughter, Eliza, born in 1826, and a son in 1832. He died as a baby, a few days before Hannah married Jonathan Sainsbury, a widower.

Following her marriage, Hannah gained some respectability and she and Jonathan had at least 7 children. Following her widowhood, Hannah moved to Easterton where she continued to work as a gardener. She had a daughter, Harriett, born 2 years after the death of her husband, so clearly she hadn't quite given up her old habits.

In 1861, she had 10 acres of land that she was gardening. She died in 1862, at the age of 61.)

12th January 1843

Inquest held by George Sylvester at West Lavington on 6th January on the body of James Sainsbury, aged 68 years, who on the day previous was giving directions in his timber yard to his men how to proceed in their work, when he leant against one of the pieces of timber and instantly fell on his face and was defunct in 10 minutes. Verdict: natural death.

1st October 1846

At West Lavington, a lad, 13 years old, named William Wyatt, who had been leading a horse to water, was found a few minutes afterwards lying on the road, insensible, with a fracture of the bones of one leg. He never recovered his consciousness to describe how the injuries were inflicted, but it is probable he received a kick from the animal, and that his head came in forcible contact with the road, producing concussion of the brain. He died in a few hours. Verdict: accidental death.

18th May 1848

Inquest at Littleton in the parish of West Lavington on Jane Goodall, aged 4 years, whose clothes became ignited by taking off the lid of the saucepan, and she died in 24 hours from the injuries she received. Verdict: accidental death.

4th January 1849

Inquest at West Lavington on James Chapman, aged 25 years. From the evidence it appears a party was shooting at a mark for a pint of beer. The deceased was standing 5 yards from Isaac Chapman, when on discharging his gun, it burst, sending fragments of both barrel and stock to a considerable distance, one of which came into contact with the left side of the head of the deceased, producing a lacerated wound of the scalp, fracturing the temporal bone, and injuring the brain. He was conveyed home in an insensible state and died the following day. Verdict: accidental death.

(James Chapman was the son of William Chapman, a labourer, and his wife Mary Green.)

10th April 1851

Inquests held by George Sylvester Esq., at Littleton in the parish of West Lavington on William Rumble, aged 20 years. From the evidence it appeared that William Beaven, carter to Mr Hooper, was proceeding from Devizes town to Lavington with his team and waggon laden with ashes, and permitted the deceased to ride at the front of the waggon. In a short time the horses started off, and the deceased was found lying in the road, blood flowing from his mouth, by William Burt of Potterne, who placed him in his trap and conveyed him home. It did not appear that the wheels had passed over him, but that death, which ensued the same evening, was caused by concussion of the brain arising from the fall. Verdict: accidental death.

(William Rumble was the son of Henry and Elizabeth Rumble.)

2nd October 1851

Inquest at West Lavington on Moses Shore, aged 24 years. James Plank was employed by Mr Sainsbury to attend on a thrashing machine, and complaining of fatigue, the deceased who was present offered to relieve him for a short time. He placed one leg in the feeding box and the other in the revolver, which made 1000 revolutions every minute, and each inflicted 6 blows by the beater, so that his limb received 6000 blows each minute.

The foot was so smashed and so jammed that it became necessary to take the machine to pieces to extricate it! Amputation was performed late in the evening, but death took place early the following morning, from shock to the nervous system and loss of blood. The accident occurred from want of care on the part of the deceased, who had been employed previously attending such machines for a considerable time. Verdict: accidental death.

(Moses Shore was the son of William Shore and Leah Goodall.)

6th April 1854

Inquest at East Lavington on William Hooper, aged 40 years. The deceased resided in Herefordshire, and came to the above place to visit a sister. On Thursday morning last, he was found partially dressed, lying on the bed, quite dead. This event was caused, according to the medical evidence, from disease of the valves of the heart. Verdict: visitation of God.

24th August 1854

Inquest at Cornbury Farm in the parish of West Lavington on George Baith (Baish), aged 10 years. The deceased placed himself on the front part of a water cart to proceed to West Lavington for water, accompanied by Robert Mead, who finding the horse's mouth sore, took off the blind halter. The horse immediately started, throwing the deceased down. He became entangled in one of the wheels, causing a fracture of the right arm, and concussion of the brain, from which death took place in a few minutes. Verdict: accidental death.

(George Baish was the son of John and Sarah Baish, nee Rumble.)

6th March 1856

Inquest at Hill Farm, West Lavington on Elizabeth Ann Langley, age 40 years. The deceased was subject to spasmodic asthma and during an attack, she fell down and expired instantly. Verdict: visitation of God.

4th February 1858

Inquest held at West Lavington on Sarah Patten, aged 65 years. The deceased retired in the evening in her usual health, and was found dead in the morning, from valvular disease of the heart. Verdict: found dead from natural causes.

12th May 1859

Two sad accidents, one of them attended with fatal consequences, occurred in the neighbourhood of Potterne late on Monday night, and rather singularly both of them were caused by the same horse. It appears that Mr Butcher of Woodbridge Mill had been attending a rook shooting at Candown Farm, and was returning home in the evening in a gig, with Mr Glass of West Lavington, when as they were descending the hill at Littleton, near Mr Abraham Newman's (A Becketts) and within a short distance of Mr Butcher's own residence, (Woodbridge Mill) the horse commenced to kicking and plunging with such violence that both Mr Butcher and Mr Glass jumped out of the gig, and in doing so sustained such injuries that they have not since been able to leave their beds. Mr Butcher, however, in the excitement of the moment, managed to get to the cottage of one of his labourers near at hand, and sent him in pursuit of the horse, which, as it belonged to a brother of Mr Butcher's at Cheverell, he supposed had taken the road to that village.

On arriving at Cheverell, however, the man found the horse had not taken that direction, and he and Mr Butcher's brother at once proceeded on horseback towards Devizes, the labourer taking the road through Worton, the brother of Mr Butcher the road towards Potterne. The latter had not gone very far before he heard a horse coming towards him at a tremendous pace, and on approaching it, taking care to keep closely at the side of the road, he recognised his own animal, with two persons behind it, one of whom, the driver, was lashing it furiously with a whip. It was with great difficulty that he kept himself and the horse upon which he rode, clear of the gig. Immediately it had passed him, he turned round, exclaiming, "What the **** are you at?" and followed the gig.

But it did not go above 100 yards further before it ran against a curb stone at the side of the road, and both its occupants were thrown violently to the ground. The horse lay as if dead, and upon going to the two persons who had been thrown out they appeared equally lifeless. One of them, who turned out to be the well-known Mr John Glass of Potterne, was utterly senseless. Having torn away the tie from around his neck, Mr Butcher laid him aside and was about to approach the other person, but a savage dog which Mr Glass had with him, precluded his doing so, and it was not until the labourer who had gone round to Worton came up, that he was able to get near him. He then found that the second person was Mr Lennard, the landlord of the George Inn at Potterne, who was quite dead. In the course of half an hour Mr Glass recovered some degree of consciousness, and both he and the deceased were removed back to Potterne, and medical aid was immediately sent for; but as far as poor Lennard was concerned, it was of no avail; he had been killed on the spot.

It appears that about 12 o'clock at night, Mr Lennard and Mr Glass were standing outside the George Inn at Potterne, neither of them we fear very sober, when Mr Butcher's horse and gig came dashing into the village. It was stopped in the street, and having been brought back to the George, the two men before mentioned got into the vehicle, for the purpose they said, of going in search of the persons who it was supposed, had been thrown out.

A shoemaker named Bull of Devizes, who was on his way to Lavington, got up behind, but the pace at which Glass drove very soon dislodged him from his perch, and he fell to the ground, paying a severe penalty for his imprudence. It was not very long after this that the accident happened, which resulted in Lennard's death. We are sorry to add that Lennard was scarcely ever sober. His wife had repeatedly told him that she should someday have him brought home dead, and the prediction of the poor woman has at last been too truly verified; and a widow and a young family have to deplore the untimely end of a drunken husband and father.

Both the deceased and Glass have met with repeated accidents arising from drink, and it is to be hoped, as the latter young man is spared, that he will for the future take a little more head to his ways. The parish of Potterne has furnished many sad instances of the results of drunkenness. We trust that the calamity of Monday night will at all events have a salutary effect upon Mr John Glass's future conduct.

An inquest was held upon the body of the deceased yesterday, by Mr Whitmarsh, when the following evidence was tendered:

Mr John Glass stated that about a quarter past 10 o'clock on Monday night he called at the George Inn, and sat down in the tap room with the deceased. A little after 12 o'clock, as he was about to go home, and was standing in the road, opposite to the inn, an empty gig drawn by a grey horse passed through the street at rather a fast pace, in the direction of the church. The horse having been stopped, was brought back to the George Inn, in a few minutes. He at first thought it was Mr Phillips's, a tea dealer in Devizes, and thinking that Mr P. was thrown out, and that he might be the means of saving his life, he said to the landlord that he would go in search of him. The landlord said he would go too, and in about a quarter of an hour from the time when the horse was first brought to the George, they started, with Glass driving.

Having proceeded about a quarter of mile out of Potterne, as far as Wick Corner, and going scarcely out of a walk that they might see any person who might have fallen into the road, the horse, from some unknown cause, commenced kicking, and then went off at a gallop. The landlord, who was still in the gig at Glass's side, at once stood up, and took hold of the near rein, which caused the horse to go in a zig-zag direction. Glass begged him not to do so, and immediately afterwards both of them were thrown out of the gig. Glass was insensible for some time, and on coming to himself, found one or two persons on the spot, and the landlord lying dead. He added that **neither he nor Lennard were intoxicated!**

Such was Mr Glass's evidence.

Mr Reuben Butcher, a farmer at Great Cheverell, was next examined. He said on Monday last he had lent the horse in question to his brother Thomas at Woodbridge Mill. A little after 12 o'clock the same night, a messenger came to him from his brother, to enquire whether the horse had come home. The witness replied that it had not, and wished to know what was the matter. The messenger then told him that his brother and Mr Glass of West Lavington, not the last witness, had been thrown out of the gig and were very much bruised, and that the horse had run away.

Upon hearing this, Butcher immediately mounted another horse and went to Woodbridge Mill, when he learnt from his brother that just as they had got to the bottom of Beckett's Hollow, the horse broke into a canter, and thence into a gallop, upon which Mr Glass endeavoured to jump out, but in doing so, hitched his foot in something in the gig, and fell violently to the ground; and that the witness's brother shared the same fate in endeavouring to get out behind.

Butcher then went in pursuit of the horse, and on coming within three quarters of a mile of Potterne, he met Mr John Glass in a gig, with the deceased, driving at a gallop. **Mr Glass was using the whip freely**. As soon as they passed, the witness turned back to go after them, when he saw the off wheel of the gig run against a curb stone at the side of the road, and the horse fell, throwing both Mr Glass and the deceased violently into the road. Glass lay insensible for nearly half an hour. Lennard was taken up quite dead.

The deceased was soon afterwards brought back to the George and a medical gentleman sent for; who at once told the deceased's friends that which they had before discovered, that poor Lennard had broken his neck.

The jury returned a verdict of accidental death.

27th March 1862

Inquest at West Lavington on Ann Kite, aged 51 years. The deceased retired in her usual health and was found dead, sitting in her chair, the following morning, from enlargement of heart and disease of its valves. Verdict: visitation of God.

12th June 1862

Inquest at West Lavington on John Davis, aged 62 years. The deceased had been employed mowing during the morning, had retired to dine, after which he was teaching a young man how to mow, when he fell to the ground and instantly expired from disease of the heart. Verdict: visitation of God.

(John Davis married Sarah Gale in 1823 and they had eight children. John was a farm labourer).

15th January 1863

Inquest at West Lavington on Jane Cruse, aged 21 years. The deceased had been confined, and died 2 hours after from syncopy, arising from internal haemorrhage. Verdict: visitation of God.

21st January 1864

Inquest at Littleton Panell in the parish of West Lavington on Alfred Coleman, aged 1 year. The deceased being left with two other children whilst his mother was gone to the well for water, applied his mouth to the spout of the kettle and swallowed some boiling water, which caused so great a degree of inflammation of the gullet and windpipe, as to prove fatal the following day. Verdict: accidental death.

24th March 1864

Inquest at Littleton Panell in the parish of West Lavington on Thomas George Staples, aged 2 months. The deceased was scalded all over the face by upsetting of a teapot containing hot tea, some of which found its way into the windpipe, producing chronic inflammation and death. Verdict: accidental death.

14th April 1864

At Littleton Panell in the parish of West Lavington on Ann Goodall, age 60 years. The deceased was employed by James Bash in the field to chop beans; she fell to the ground and died instantly from serious apoplexy. Verdict: visitation of God.

13th October 1864

A carter in the employ of Mrs Lush of West Lavington was accidentally killed last Friday afternoon. The poor fellow, whose name was George Hill aged 54, had been sent by the bailiff with 3 horses and a waggon to fetch a load of hay. He was accompanied by a little carter boy named Kyte, and had passed through Littleton, and had reached the top of what is known as Beckett's Hollow, when the horses, which were very fresh, shied at something in the road and commenced plunging. The boy who was with the team, Hill being in the waggon, seized the first horse by the head, but was instantly hurled back against the bank, and thus fortunately escaped injury. Hill immediately jumped from the waggon, and was seen to have hold of some part of the harness, but whether this gave way, or whether he was knocked down by the horses, which were by this time all plunging together, is not known. At all events he fell in the road, and both the near wheels passed directly over his neck and chest, killing him on the spot.

The horses, finding themselves uncontrolled now, dashed off at a furious pace along the turnpike road, one of them, according to the statement of an eye witness, throwing a shoe as high as the top of the trees. They continued at a full gallop until they reached Woodbridge Mill, the gate to which chanced to be open. Turning through this they ran on to the mill, where they were stopped, without having done the least injury either to themselves or the waggon.

Poor Hill had, we understand, been for many years in the employ of Mrs Lush and her late husband, and was a well conducted, steady man. He has left a widow and several children, the latter however are all grown up. An inquest was held upon his body on Monday last, and a verdict of accidental death was returned.

13th April 1865

Inquest held at West Lavington on the 10th inst. before G. Sylvester Esq., on the body of a child aged 18 months, named Harriet Giddings, who died suddenly on the previous Saturday from congestion of the lungs brought on by a violent cold. Verdict: died by visitation of God.

11th January 1868

Fatal Exposure to the inclemency of the weather:

An inquest was held at West Lavington before Mr Sylvester, coroner, on the body of John Weeks, aged 55. The deceased and his nephew on New Year's Eve visited some friends at Upavon, and were returning home on the afternoon of the next day, the deceased appearing in good health, and having partaken of a hearty dinner, when near the Charlton Cat, he went down in a stooping position in the trap, and afterwards commenced snoring.

The nephew, thinking that he was sound asleep, did not interfere with him, but when they arrived at the Bridge Inn at West Lavington, found he was dead. The surgeon was of the opinion that the deceased had been intemperate, and consequently lost nervous energy, and that being exposed to extreme cold he died in a state of exhaustion. Verdict: died from exposure to the inclemency of the weather.

(John Weeks married Sarah Draper in Bath in 1849. They had a daughter, Jane, born in 1850. The 1851 census shows John was a farmer of 78 acres at that time, living at Connops, but in 1861, he was shown as an agricultural labourer).

17th March 1870

Inquest at Littleton Panell in the parish of West Lavington on Henry Lane, aged 6 weeks. The infant was placed on the bed on Friday evening in good health but was found dead on the following morning with a livid countenance and other symptoms indicating suffocation. Verdict: accidental death.

5th May 1870

Inquest at West Lavington on Jane Davis, aged 44 years. The deceased had varicose veins in the legs, and having stood all day at the wash tub, one of the veins in the evening burst and discharged an immense quantity of blood. A bandage was placed round the leg, but was ineffectual in stopping the bleeding and death took place in 20 minutes. Verdict: syncope caused by haemorrhage from a diseased vein in the leg.

(Jane was married to William Davis, a Chelsea Pensioner. They had 6 children, the youngest of whom was only 2 at the time of Jane's death. The 1871 census shows William was managing to keep his family together, presumably with help from his elder children).

22nd December 1870

Inquest at West Lavington on Sarah Jane Goddard, aged 9 months. The mother of the deceased went into the garden leaving her on the floor, and when she returned she found her in flames. Charles Hitchcock Esq. MD was of the opinion that the deceased died from the effect of the burns. Verdict: accidental death.

Chapter Seven
Manslaughter

26th August 1858

Death Caused by Negligent Driving

On Monday evening last considerable excitement was produced in Market Lavington, in consequence of Edward Beaven of Stert being taken into custody by the police, charged with having occasioned the death of a child about 4 years of age, the son of a poor man of Shrewton, through the furious driving of a pony and cart near Cornbury Mill. The poor man, it appeared, had sent his 3 children to Littleton, to be taken care of by his wife's sister, named Bartlett, the mother being an inmate of the Salisbury Infirmary. But it being feast day at Lavington they had come home with the Bartletts, and were returning to Littleton in the evening, in charge of a girl 11 years of age.

When near the mill, a horse and cart was heard rapidly approaching. The girl, alarmed for their safety, gathered up the little ones and placed them on a flint heap at the side of the road, but she had hardly done so, before the vehicle ran against the stones, knocked down the eldest of the 3 children, and killed him on the spot.

Beavan was pursued and brought back by a person named Giddings who happened to be passing at the time, and the dead body being placed in his cart, was carried to the Cross Keys at Littleton, and Beavan was taken into custody to await the result of the coroner's inquest.

This took place on the following Tuesday, before G. Sylvester Esq., when the prisoner was brought into the room by Superintendent Wolfe, who requested to be allowed to examine witnesses, in order to prove the furious driving. But to this the coroner objected on the ground that the death of the deceased might have been caused by an accident. The case was thereupon left in the hands of the parish constable. The only evidence produced being that of a man and a woman who were near the spot, together with that of the girl, and the result of the enquiry was a verdict of accidental death.

The verdict has created much dissatisfaction, and it is said that the matter will undergo a searching investigation before the Magistrates, as the habit of furious driving has become a most intolerable nuisance. It was stated by one witness that Beavan was driving at the rate of 8 and by another at the rate of 10 miles an hour at the time of the accident. It further appeared that he had been drinking at Market Lavington for 2-3 hours previously, and was considerably the worse for liquor; and that his driving through Lavington Street, previous to the accident, was extremely dangerous, several people having to get out of the way, for fear of being driven over.

2nd September 1858

Inquest taken before George Sylvester Esq. at Littleton in the parish of West Lavington on John Couldrick, aged 3 years. Margaret Hobbs deposed:

"I was proceeding to Market Lavington, near Cornbury Mill, I saw a man driving a pony in a cart coming towards Littleton at a fast rate. He was driving with reins, and was endeavouring to pull up. I looked round and saw a child, the deceased, lying on the road. I picked him up and found he was quite dead. At this part of the road it was very dark from some trees growing on one side. This occurred last evening, August 23rd, at half past 9 o'clock."

Mary Ann Early, aged 11 years deposed:

"I was returning last evening about 9 o'clock from Market Lavington, and had the care of the deceased, John Coultrick, and two younger children. A trap and horse were coming very fast down the hill towards Cornbury Mill, driven by a man whom I did not know. He appeared to be endeavouring to stop the horse, which was unmanageable from the britching of the harness having broken. I placed the deceased on a flint heap at the side of the road, the wheel knocked him down and killed him on the spot. The man pulled up as quickly as he could, and conveyed the deceased to the Cross Keys Inn at Littleton."

Thomas Giddings deposed:

"I was proceeding towards Market Lavington. I passed a cart and horse driven by Edward Beaven of Stert Mill at the rate of 8 miles an hour. He was trying to pull the horse up, but the britching became undone and slipped down, allowing the front of the cart to irritate the hinder parts of the horse as to render him unmanageable. It was dark at this part of the road, and another vehicle was passing at the time, obliging Beaven to draw to the side of the road towards the children. If the harness had not given way I am of the opinion the accident would not have occurred."

William Brown Pepler, surgeon, deposed:

"I was called last evening to visit the deceased. I found him dead from concussion of the brain. There was no external injury."

Verdict: accidentally killed.

17th March 1859

Charge of Manslaughter Against Edward Beaven

Edward Beaven, a miller of Stert, about 24 years of age, was indicted for killing a child named John Coldrake at Market Lavington on the 23rd of August.

The charge sought to be established against the prisoner was that he had caused the death of the child whilst driving a pony in a trap at a reckless pace and whilst in a state of intoxication.

Seeing the prisoner coming along at a furious rate, a girl who had the charge of 3 children, one of whom was the deceased, put them upon a heap of flints by the side of the road, where the wheel caught one of them and killed him upon the spot.

Several witnesses were called on behalf of the prosecution, with the view of showing that the pace at which the prisoner was driving at the time was not only furious, but that the pony was urged to the top of its speed without any attempt to stop it.

The first witness was Robert Carter, who said that he was standing by Mr Read's the chemist at Market Lavington, about three quarters of a mile from where the accident happened, when the prisoner passed at a gallop, and that although he was holding the reins pretty tight in the hand, he was not attempting to pull them. The next witness was a woman named Sarah Bartlett, but whose evidence was not worth much, as she was proved to have been intoxicated at the time. She stated that she saw the prisoner driving the pony as fast as it could go, and hitting it at the time with the butt-end of a whip.

A third witness, named Sloper, also deposed to seeing the prisoner driving the pony at a gallop, but could not say whether he was trying to pull in or not. A fourth witness, a Mrs Brown, who was walking on the road from Market Lavington to West Lavington, when she saw the prisoner coming in a trap at a tremendous pace, and was so frightened that she got as close to the bank at the side of the road as she could possibly get, to avoid being run over, and even then the prisoner's trap went within two inches of her. Mr Webb, a miller, also deposed to seeing the prisoner driving as fast as he could make the horse go, and whilst doing so, he distinctly heard him urging the horse on, when within 60 or 70 yards of where the child was killed.

For the defence however, it was attempted to be shown that the pony had taken fright, that the prisoner had lost control over it, and that the accident was the result of misadventure, but the evidence which was to support this conclusion was of a rather contradictory character.

A woman named Hobbs for instance swore most positively that she was close by when the child was killed, and that the prisoner was at the time merely driving at a trot, and not very fast. A boy named Duck on the other hand said that he saw the horse take fright and run away some time before it came to where the children were; whilst another witness, a Mrs Coleman, stated that she saw the horse going at a gallop, and the prisoner trying to pull it, in a part of the road before it came to where the boy said he saw it first start off.

The fact that the pony was not beyond control, if the prisoner had been in a condition to exercise it, was shown by a man named Thomas Giddings. He, it appeared, was driving a trap in an opposite direction to that in which the prisoner was coming, and seeing as he said, the 'caddling' way in which he was driving, he pulled in at the side of the road to give him room to pass, just at the spot where the child was killed. Immediately upon seeing what had occurred he turned his trap round, drove after the prisoner, and brought him back. He was not he said at the time, driving at the rate of more than 8 miles an hour, and the presumption that he was drunk was gathered from the witness Hobbs, who said he appeared so both from his talk and his walk.

The judge, who took great pains in summing up the case, evidently considered that the charge had been brought home to the prisoner, and went so far as to remark that there was no excuse whatever for his having run over the child. That he had **tried** to do it, was not suggested; if he had done so, he would have been guilty of murder. It was quite sufficient to show that he was at the time driving so negligently and incautiously, as by it to cause the death of the child, and of this his Lordship seemed to entertain very little doubt.

The jury, however, returned a verdict of not guilty.

This verdict was received by several of the prisoner's friends in Court with applause. Upon which the Judge remarked that if anybody was caught expressing approbation or disapprobation, especially at the verdict of the Jury, he would commit them to gaol immediately.

Chapter Eight
Poisoning at West Lavington

9th August 1866

Mysterious Case

Three relatives from Avebury dined with Mrs Gale and her son at her house at Littleton, near West Lavington on Sunday fortnight. Soon after dinner all were taken ill and violently sick. The young man and his mother have continued ill ever since, and on Tuesday morning the son died. The relatives had sufficiently recovered to return home. Two or three children who had eaten some of the plum pudding, of which the party had partaken, were also attacked with vomiting, etc.

Yesterday Mr Sylvester held an inquest on the body of the young man, Edward Gale, and Mr Pepler, the surgeon gave evidence of some sugar found in the house, some of which had been used in making the pudding, containing arsenic. A small packet of arsenic was found in the clock case, but how any of it came to be in the sugar is a mystery. Edward Gale might, like the rest, have recovered from the first attack, but he seems to have taken some of the sugar daily in brandy and water since.

Both he and his mother denied having any poison in the house.

16th August 1866

Another Death from Poisoning at West Lavington

Our paper last week contained a short account of a mysterious case of poisoning that had occurred at West Lavington resulting in the death of a young man named Edward Gale. We have now to record the death, from the same cause, of Edward Gale's mother; and our only wonder is, on learning of the circumstances which have since transpired, that more persons have not fallen victims.

Mrs Gale and her son were, it appears, natives of Avebury, having come to reside in West Lavington about 8 years ago, and it was on the occasion of a visit from some relatives from Avebury, last Sunday 3 weeks, that the poison which has since been detected commenced its deadly work.

A Mrs Chivers had previously been staying with the Gales, and it was in expectation of her husband on the Sunday, to fetch his wife home, that a good dinner was prepared, and among other things, that a large plum pudding was made on the previous night. In the making of this pudding, Mrs Gale, Mrs Chivers, and a Miss Baker, the intended wife of Edward Gale the son, all had a hand. The sugar with which it was sweetened was taken from a large glazed brown earthen jar, which had not been entirely emptied for some time, but the whole contents of which were now turned out into a basin. That which was not used in the pudding was set aside for subsequent use.

The pudding was boiled the same night and it appears that after it was taken out of the pot, in order to make it stand level upon the dish, a small bit was cut off, which Mrs Gale and Mrs Chivers ate. They had not however swallowed it long, before they experienced unpleasant sensations, but they felt pretty well again the next morning, and all sat down to dinner and partook of the pudding.

The only person who does not appear to have ate heartily of it was Chivers, the husband who had just come from Avebury, and the brother of Mrs Gale, but he was so affected by what he had taken that he afterwards threw up the whole of his dinner. The rest were all violently sick, and Mr Pepler the surgeon was sent for to see Mrs Gale the same evening.

No suspicion was then entertained as to the cause of the sickness, and for 2 or 3 days afterwards Mrs Gale appeared to be going on pretty well, when she again became worse, her stomach ejecting everything that she took. In this way she went on, sometimes a little better, then again violently sick, as she partook more or less of the sugar with which the gruel and tea given to her were sweetened, until her whole system had become so impregnated with some then unknown poisonous agency, that she died on Friday last, her son having died the previous Tuesday, after partaking, like his mother, of the sugar, as it was required up to within a few days of his death.

It was at first thought by the doctor that the illness of the mother and son might have arisen from the use of a copper pot, but from the severity of the symptoms, he became satisfied that it was caused by something of a more malignant character, and at his first visit he requested them to throw away everything they had been using. The last thing suspected was the sugar; and it was not until this had been nearly all used, and after the young man's death, that Miss Baker said to Mr Pepler: "I think I know what has caused this; I believe it was the sugar, for I took some of it and was sick afterwards."

The whole contents of the basin had then been used, in sweetening the tea, gruel and brandy and water that had been given to the sick patients; but there was some still adhering to the bottom of the large earthen jar, and upon this being analysed by Mr Pepler, it was found to contain a considerable quantity of arsenic. In short there is now no doubt that the whole party were poisoned by the sugar that was thrown out of the jar when the pudding was made, and the death of Mrs Gale and her son is to be attributed to their having continued to use this sugar until it had done its work.

The question which naturally arises is: how came the arsenic in the sugar? It was well known to Mrs Chapman, a neighbour, that Mrs Gale was in the habit of using arsenic to kill mice about her premises; in fact a small packet of the poison has since been found in the clock case; and the only way in which it can be accounted for in the sugar is this:

It appears that about 4 months ago, Mrs Gale and her son moved house, and the large jar in which the sugar is kept being empty, a number of packets were placed in it for convenience of removal. It is suggested that one of these packets might have been a packet containing arsenic, and that after their removal, sugar was put in the jar without cleaning it. At all events, no injurious result followed the use of the sugar until that which was at the bottom of the jar was turned out. Mrs Gale, it is said, generally replenished her stock before it was quite exhausted. It was only when the entire contents of the jar were emptied, and that which had remained at the bottom for 3 or 4 months was used, that any ill effects showed themselves, and the presence of arsenic in the hard particles of sugar which still adhered to the bottom of the jar would seem to favour this suggestion.

One thing is quite certain, that both Mrs Gale and her son have died from the effects of arsenic; and the fact that everyone who is known to have had any hands with the sugar partook of it, and suffered from so doing, would dispel any idea of the poisoning having been wilfully occasioned. The only person who does not appear to have partaken of the sugar was the neighbour named Chapman who came in to attend the Gales; but the fact of her having cut off a slice of the pudding and given to each of her children as they were going to school, removes any suspicion of collusion on her part. The children, it may be stated, were both ill afterwards.

An inquest was, as we stated in our last, held upon Edward Gale, the son, on Wednesday; and on Friday last another inquest was held upon the body of the mother, before Mr Coroner Sylvester, and a respectable jury.

Several witnesses were examined; among them Mary Hibberd, who said:

"On Tuesday 7ᵗʰ I went to attend on Mrs Gale who was then very ill in bed, and I didn't leave her until her death. She complained much of a pain in her chest, her eyes were very red, and she was not sensible for any length of time together. She had lost the use of her legs, and was much relaxed the day before she died. I lifted her out of bed 3 times on that day, as she had no power whatever to help herself. I saw Elizabeth Chapman take a parcel from the clock case. It was marked 'Poison'. I cannot say how long it is ago since I was looking after Mrs Gale, with Mrs Chapman, at the cottage she used to live in, but I recollect then seeing what I believe to be the same parcel in the clock case. I know Mrs Gale used to put poison about at the other cottage to kill mice, and I was cautioned about my cat in consequence, lest she should be killed as well as the mice."

John Chivers of Avebury, brother of Mrs Gale, the deceased, and one of the party who partook of the pudding, said:

"I partook of some of the pudding on the Sunday, but only a very small quantity, and 2 hours afterwards I felt some queer sensations. The whole of us had been invited to tea at a friend's house that same afternoon, but they were all too ill to go except myself, and about 7 o'clock I was taken so bad that I threw up the whole dinner I had eaten. The deceased lived next door to me at Avebury before she came to Littleton. At that time I was in the habit of using large quantities of arsenic for dipping sheep, but I don't remember giving or selling any to my sister, nor do I remember her having asked me for any. Indeed I have never given any arsenic to anyone, although asked for it on several occasions."

(It seems more than probable, however, that Mrs Gale possessed herself of the arsenic which was found on her premises whilst she was living at Avebury, as that which was in the clock case was wrapped in an old shop paper of

Mr Gundry's, in use several years ago, when Mr Gundry used to supply the neighbourhood of Avebury with groceries.)

Mrs Chapman stated that since the day the pudding was partaken of, she had been in attendance upon the Gales, and had sweetened the gruel and tea she had given to Mrs Gale, and brandy and water which she had made for Edward Gale, with the sugar from the basin, until it was all gone, when she sent some sugar from her own house, in consequence of Mrs Gale's jar being empty. She also deposed to having given some of the pudding to her children as they were going to school, and to their both being ill afterwards.

Mr Pepler, surgeon, said:

"On the 22nd July, the same day the party had partaken of the pudding, I was called in to see Mrs Gale. She was very sick, but not so bad as some of the others. She went on very well for 2 or 3 days, when from some unaccountable cause, she became worse and ejected everything she swallowed. I had attended her a long time previously for dropsy. She died yesterday morning.

"For 2 or 3 days before her death, she was very restless and wandering, which I attribute to her having taken arsenic. I analysed some sugar which was taken from a jar in the deceased's house, and found it to contain arsenic. At my first visit, I thought the illness of the parties might have arisen from the use of a copper pot; but from the severity of the case, I became satisfied it must be something more, and I requested that everything they had been using might be destroyed. Miss Baker said to me after Edward Gale's death, 'I think I know what has caused this'. I asked her what? She said, 'The sugar'. I asked her why? 'Because I took some of it', she said, 'and I felt sick afterwards'."

The coroner said there could be no doubt that the death of Mrs Gale had arisen from the same cause as that of her son, that both had died from taking arsenic. It was proved that arsenic had been kept in the clock case, and that it was used by Mrs Gale to destroy the mice about her premises; and it was just possible that in her infirm state, she was not quite so cautious in its use as she ought to have been, and that some of it might have been inadvertently left about, and got intermixed with the sugar. He thought therefore the jury would be disposed to consider the deceased had come by her death by the accidental taking of arsenic.

The jury, however, rather demurred to this, and after a long consultation, they said it was the opinion of many of them that the enquiry should be adjourned to a future day.

The coroner said he did not see that any good was likely to arise from an adjournment, and a good deal of altercation ensued when Mr Supt Wolfe observed that it might be satisfactory to the jury to know that if the inquest were closed an active enquiry would be kept up by the police, and if anything should transpire criminating any party whatever, that the law would be put in force.

With this assurance the jury expressed themselves satisfied, and the verdict suggested by the coroner was returned.

Chapter Nine
The Lavington Abduction
22nd September 1864

Considerable excitement was caused in the neighbourhood of Lavington last week, by a discovery made on Wednesday morning that the daughter of Mr Box, the engineer, had left her father's home late on the previous night, and absconded with a man named Boucher. The young lady, whose name is Catherine Alice is not yet 16 years of age, whilst her paramour is about 32, and from what has since transpired, it would seem that the whole affair was concerted by a woman named Beard, at Market Lavington, in whose house Boucher lodged, and to whose connivance the painful result to the family of Mr Box is attributed.

It appears that late on Tuesday night, after it was supposed by the family that she was in bed, Boucher met Miss B. at her father's gate, and that both of them went straight to the house of Mrs Beard, where they stayed for three hours, and then went away in the direction of Woodborough. The discovery of the flight by Mr and Mrs Box was not made until the following morning, when on searching their daughter's room some pieces of paper were found, one of which was directed to her father, and informed him that she had gone to Poulshot to see her uncle, and that she was going from thence to Bristol.

Mr Box upon this immediately went to Poulshot, but finding that he had been misled, he returned to Devizes, and made enquiry at the railway station whether anyone answering the description of his daughter had been seen there; and unable to gather any tidings of her here, he acquainted the police with what had happened, and Mr Superintendent Wolfe soon discovered that Boucher, who had been lodging for the previous fortnight at the White Hart Inn in Devizes, and who, it is well known among his associates had been keeping up a correspondence with

Miss Box, and had been seen about with her at different times, had left suddenly on the day previous.

On making further enquiries, it was ascertained that a woman had been to the White Hart overnight and fetched Boucher away in a trap, and that a conversation between them had been overheard, which left little doubt as to the object of his sudden departure. Upon this Mr Wolfe went to Lavington, and proceeded at once to the house of Mrs Beard, for, from the description that had been given of the woman who had fetched Boucher away from the White Hart, it was at once suspected that she was that person.

Mrs Beard however pretended at first to be entirely ignorant of the matter, but finding that more was known of her complicity in the affair than she was aware of, she acknowledged that both Boucher and Miss B. had been to her house overnight; but she said that Miss Box had left at 10 and Boucher at 11 o'clock, and that she knew nothing more about them, nor where they had gone.

It was subsequently ascertained however that they had both walked to Woodborough on the previous night; that they had called at a cottage there about 2 o'clock in the morning; that they had stayed there until the arrival of the first up-train, and that they had then taken tickets for Paddington.

Upon this Mr Box proceeded to London, and the same night circulated information through the police districts, so far as he was able, with a view to tracing the destination of the fugitives. No tidings however could be heard of them, but on the following morning a letter was received by Mr House, the landlord of the Green Dragon Inn at Market Lavington, whom Boucher appears to have made trustee over the little property he possessed, requesting that a post office order for £10 might be sent to him immediately to a certain address in London, as he was about to be married and had got no money.

Mr House of course lost no time in communicating the intelligence to Mr Box's son, who started off without a moment's delay to London, and on his arrival proceeded to the place named in Boucher's letter. He found however that the parties had left there, but he was directed by the person belonging to the lodging house where they had passed the previous night, to a coffee shop not far off, where he found Boucher and his sister sitting at a table together in a room by themselves.

Mr Box junior immediately collared Boucher, and held him until the arrival of the police, when he was taken to the police station, Miss Box accompanying him, and on the following day they were brought before the Magistrates at the Marylebone Court.

From thence Boucher was ordered to be taken to Devizes, and on the following day he was brought before the Rev A. Smith at the Magistrate's office in this town. But before any charge was gone into against him, Mr Superintendent Wolfe obtained a warrant against the woman Beard, and she was apprehended at Lavington and brought into Devizes, in time for both her and Boucher to be remanded until Thursday. Bail however was afterwards accepted for her appearance, her husband in £100, and two sureties in £50 each, and she was discharged. But Boucher, who was not able to procure bail, was sent to gaol, where we understand he has since had an attack of delirium tremens, a thing not to be wondered at, considering the dissolute life he has been leading for a long time past.

It appears that after Miss Box was missed, her mother found 2 letters in the bedroom in which she slept, written by Mrs Beard, suggesting the time and the mode whereby it would be convenient for her to get away, so that her friends might know nothing about it. Indeed, from what Miss Box has since herself confessed, there cannot be a shadow of doubt that Mrs Beard has been at the bottom of the whole affair. The girl says that she should never have gone to her house at all, had she not been induced to do so by this woman; that she was passing one day alone, when Mrs Beard came out and asked her to come in, telling her that there was somebody inside who wanted to see her; that she went in, and was shown into a room, where she found Boucher, who in the most impassioned way made love to her, and that afterwards she was a frequent visitor at Mrs Beard's house. It was Mrs Beard who dictated one, and wrote the other, letter which appear in the police report of the examination in London; it was at Mrs Beard's house that all the arrangements were made for them to get away together. Mrs Beard promised to do everything in her power to assist them in the elopement; and that by way of carrying out this promise, she came into Devizes on the Tuesday evening and conveyed Boucher to Lavington, promising while passing the girl's father's house, to give some pre-arranged signal whereby she might know that it was all right. That shortly after the family had gone to bed, she packed up her things, and in company with Boucher, who was waiting outside her father's gate, went to Mrs Beard's house, and there remained with Boucher, until their departure for Woodborough.

It further appears that after Mr Superintendent Wolfe had been to Mrs Beard's on Wednesday, Mrs Beard wrote a letter to Miss Box in London, informing her of what was going on, that her papa and mamma were in London searching for her, and that the police had been sent the other way; at the same time blaming her for leaving letters behind which she, Beard, had written, arranging the elopement; and telling her to keep quiet, or it might be the means of getting her, Beard, transported.

Fig. 3

A host of other letters have since been found, showing that a secret correspondence had been going on between Miss Box and Boucher for several months past; and that Miss Box was quite aware of the intemperate habits of the man, a fact which, it may be remembered, was made apparent at the last Petty Sessions held in Devizes, when Boucher was fined 10 shillings and costs for having been found by the police helplessly drunk in Market Lavington on the Sunday fortnight previously. He is, it is stated, a Trowbridge man, and had been living at Lavington for several months before the elopement took place, almost always in a state of intoxication, a habit which his means, unfortunately gave him the opportunity of indulging, as he is said to have private means amounting to about 23s or 24s a week.

Mrs Beard is the wife of a little shopkeeper at Lavington. She was formerly one of the Hamptons of Potterne.

Lyn Dyson

Report of Boucher's Examination before the Magistrate in London

The following report of the prisoner Boucher's examination before the Magistrate on his being taken into custody in London, appeared in Saturday's morning papers:

A well-dressed man, with a profusion of moustache and beard, and who gave his name as James Boucher aged 32 of no occupation, was charged before the Magistrate at Marylebone Police Court on Friday last, with unlawfully decoying and taking away Catherine Alice Box, under the age of sixteen, she being only 15 years and 9 months, out of the possession and against the will of her father and mother, William Box and Sarah Anne Box of Market Lavington, near Devizes. He was further charged with stealing a quantity of wearing apparel, valued at £8, the property of William Box, the father.

William Box said: "I reside at Market Lavington, Wiltshire. I am a practical engineer. I have seen the prisoner as a resident at Devizes, and he has also lodged at a public house in Market Lavington. On Tuesday morning I missed my daughter. Her birthday, which will complete her 16th year, is in December next. I made enquiries about the house and found a little note in pencil in which she said she had gone to Poulshot, a village near. I went there, but could not find her, and went on to Devizes Station and telegraphed a description of my daughter up and down the line. I heard that she had been seen with a man, but could not imagine that he was the prisoner. Sometime after I heard of her at Woodborough. I went there and learnt that my daughter and the prisoner had walked from Market Lavington to that place, a distance of eight or nine miles, and the prisoner was seen carrying a bundle of clothes, and that they had taken the express train to London. From what was told me by the Superintendent of Police, I came to London, and went to Scotland Yard, where I lodged information, and had her description printed. Last night I saw her at Paddington Green police station."

The daughter Catherine was next called; she was very juvenile in appearance, and wore a small straw hat with a black lace fall. She was crying and averted her gaze from the prisoner. She stated, "I have known the prisoner for about 9 months. On Tuesday last I left home with him. He came to the gate of our house; he did not come in. He asked me if I was ready, and we went to Market Lavington and to Mrs Beard's there. We stayed 3 hours there; we were to have driven to Woodborough Station, but the horse fell and we had to walk. We got someone to carry our bundle. We called at an inn, but they refused to accommodate us, and we had to go to some man's cottage, and from there we came to Paddington. We went to No.1 London Street. We remained there one night, and yesterday my brother came and found us out."

Mr Mansfield said there was quite sufficient evidence for him to order the prisoner to be taken to Devizes, there to be brought before the justices.

At the house No.1 London Street, the Inspector took from the prisoner the following letter:

Broadway House, Lavington.

Ever dearest Jim,

I have just come home, and have walked fast. You know what is the matter, and my head aches, and I feel so sick. I can't write, but dearest can I get away. I will see you on Thursday. Bessie is coming in tomorrow. She will tell you that your deeds have proved fatal at last. But you love me. I am all right.

With fond love and kisses,
believe me ever yours,
Kate.

The letter was addressed to Mr Boucher near New Park Street, Devizes.

Broadway House.

Dearest Jim,

Long and anxious do I wait for tomorrow night. Do not come to Lavington until it is dark. I wish you to go to Mrs Beard's about 8 o'clock, and not go out anywhere after. People will not have the least idea where we are. Bessie's brother is coming in tomorrow. If anything is said he will speak for you. Oh Jim, you are in my thoughts all night! Could I but sleep and let you be absent from my mind! But darling we shall be together on Thursday evening at this time. Excuse greatest haste. Do come tomorrow night. Don't I love to be Mrs Boucher! It is my only wish to know that I am that. Bessie has been so kind; she has been a mother to me, but you I look upon as everything. Tell Mr Martin to keep quiet.

Accept, darling Jim, the most affectionate love from your intended little Kitty.

P.S. Could a girl long for anything more than I do to see you tomorrow? Mrs Beard will tell you the time I am coming and all about it.

Two letters were also produced, one written by the prisoner, and the other by the girl, asking Mrs House of the Green Dragon, Market Lavington, to send up a post office order for £10. This letter Mrs House placed in the hands of the young lady's brother.

Prisoner, when removed, seemed as if seized with a fit of ague, he shook so violently.

29th September 1864

On Thursday last, Boucher, the man charged with the abduction of Miss Catherine Alice Box from her father's house at Lavington, and a Mrs Beard, who is said to have aided and abetted the abduction, were brought up for reexamination at the Magistrate's office in Devizes, before Mr Locke and the Rev Dr Wilkinson.

Mr Wittey appeared on behalf of Boucher, and Mr Wilton of Bath on behalf of Mrs Beard.

The first witness examined was Mr Box, the father of the young lady, who deposed to all his family having been at home on the Tuesday evening when the flight took place. He and Mrs Box went to bed a little after 10 o'clock, his daughter Catherine Alice having gone to bed about half an hour previously. On the following morning they were informed that she was missing, and directly afterwards a scrap of paper was found in her room by Mrs Box, on which were written these words:

'Good-bye. I am gone to Poulshot. Care not about me. I shall be happy. I am going to be married'.

On reading this communication, Mr Box immediately started off to Poulshot, and finding that his daughter had not been there, he went in pursuit of her in another direction, and ultimately found her in London, as detailed in our paper last week.

Mrs Box was next examined. She deposed to having seen her daughter safe, undressed, and in bed a few minutes before 10 o'clock on the night the elopement took place, and to subsequently finding the note already read, and also two others, which were handed to Mr Superintendent Wolfe the same day. These notes were now put in and read.

The first, it will be observed, is a letter from Miss Box to Mrs Beard:

Broadway House

My dearest friend Bessy,

Thanks for your sincere kindness to me since I have known you. I am sorry I shall never be able to repay you in any way for it. If I come up to-day I am in hope to see you, and be advised by you what to do, as I am miserable and Jim knows what an end he has brought me to. I thought I was to be Mrs Boucher when he said that I so many times should. You can guess what trouble I am into, and now whatever you think I had better do I will; but dearest Bessy, if you know where he is will you, for my sake, send to him and ask him to return and have me. If he will let me have only time to get what clothes I must have, I am ready. I will pay any expense to convey any message or letter to him, for as soon as Papa and Ma find out what is the matter, they will turn me out of doors entirely; then Jim will be gone. Where can I go? What can I do? Oh! Could you only think the anxiety of my mind you would be a friend. Doubtless you will. I am that ill I cannot tell what to do. I can't eat or do anything; but Bessy, if you will write to him or tell me where to write to, I will pay every expense it may cost you. Do, dearest, write to him for me. Beg him to come back, if only for two days. DO PLEASE DO IT.

Please accept the album enclosed, with my very fond love. The likeness sent is a very bad one, but you shall have another in a few days. Be a true friend. Do send to him. He, I hear, is with the people belonging to the Theatre. Tell him it is I that want him. Do not say a word that I have told you what is the matter.

The following is Mrs Beard's letter:

Dearest Kate,

I shall be happy to see you on Sunday, and I should think that Tuesday would do very nicely, but it would not be wise of you to leave until all are gone to bed Monday night. We will talk about the rest Sunday as the boy is in a hurry.

Yours truly,
Bessie.

Catherine Alice Box herself was then called. She proceeded to detail the whole correspondence that had taken place between her and Mrs Beard. The first time she became acquainted with her was, she said about the latter part of July or early in August, when, as she was passing up Lavington Street, Mrs Beard called her in and asked her if she was not fond of Mr Boucher. She replied that she was not, but that she had spoken to him several times. I believe, said Mrs Beard, your friends object to your keeping company with him; but if I was you I would do so, and if I could not do so by day I would by night, and anything I can do to assist you I should be pleased to do.

Numbers of letters after this passed to and fro, between Mrs Beard and the witness, sometimes as many as 3 or 4 in the course of a day; and so matters went on until a week before the elopement, when according to Miss Box's statement, Mrs Beard undertook to go into Devizes and see Boucher, who was then living in this town, and get him to come to Lavington, and promised that she would then drive them as far as Woodborough Station. That on the Tuesday evening, the 13th September, Mrs Beard so far fulfilled her engagement by going into Devizes and fetching Boucher; and that the witness on her return was made aware of the fact by a preconcerted signal from Mrs Beard, who, in passing her father's house in a trap with Boucher at about 9 o'clock, waved a white handkerchief and said, "Good night! Come up! I've got him!"

A little while after her father and mother had gone to bed, she got up and packed a quantity of her clothing, and then went out to the front gate where she met Boucher. They both proceeded to Mrs Beard's where they remained to between 12 and 1 at night, but in consequence of Mrs Beard's pony having fallen down on its way back from Devizes, she was unable to convey them on as at first intended, and that it was then proposed that they should walk.

They accordingly set off on foot, Boucher carrying the bundle until they got to Eastcott, where he called upon a man named Dowse, who afterwards carried the bundle for them. They went as far as the Wells' beer-house at Chirton Hollow where they called upon the landlord to get up and let them in, with Miss Box peremptorily insisting upon his doing so as they were travellers. Mr Wells however could not be prevailed upon to come down stairs, and the party were compelled to trudge on to Woodborough, where they induced a cottager to take them in and where they remained until just before the first up train arrived, when Miss Box took 2 tickets for Paddington, Boucher supplying her with the money.

On reaching London they took up their quarters at the Great Western Coffee House, No.1 London Street, and during the day Boucher went to a jeweller's shop to purchase a ring preparatory to their being married. Being short of cash however, he found himself under the necessity of writing to Mr House, the landlord of the Green Dragon Inn, Market Lavington, whom he had some time previously made temporary trustee of the little property he had, asking Mr H. to remit him a post office order for £10. Miss Box wrote on the same paper to Mrs House, saying that they were to be sure to send the money as Boucher was not drunk, and as he had now got a wife she would be sure to take care of his money for him. Curiously enough, however, she added at the end of this note that they intended to be married the next day.

Miss Box went on further to state that they removed from the Great Western coffee-house during the day, to No.16 in the same street, where they were found by her brother on the following day, and when Boucher was given in charge and brought before one of the London Magistrates, as stated last week.

Letters found in Boucher's possession were then put in and read.

The following is a letter from Mrs Beard to Miss Box, in reply to one Miss Box sent to her, after the elopement, and which, it appears, Mrs Beard has admitted to be her handwriting, although it bears no signature:

Dear Mrs B.,

I received your kind letter this morning, but I shall not have anything to say about the money. We have had Mr Wolfe here about you, and I am blamed for everything. They said that I was the cause of it. You know that I am not. I tried to be a friend to you, and then you went away and left my letters in the house, which I think was very wrong of you. Wolfe so frightened me that I have done nothing but cry, and I feel very ill about it. Do declare that I knew nothing. I said it would not be wise for them to know that you were coming up to tell me. Be on my side and I will still be your friend. I may be transported if you tell them that I was the cause of it. Your papa and mama is in London pursuing you, and Wolfe is gone the other way, but if you are married they cannot hurt you; but you must show your certificate to prove it. So be aware of that.

Signed by, and may God bless you.
Accept our love from your affectionate friend.
Please burn this for my sake. Do now.

The following is also one of Mrs Beard's epistles:

Dear Kate,

You must not trouble about Monday; that will be all right. Martin is going in with him, for he told me so and so is Farmer and House. The boy is in such a hurry.

Kind love,
Yours Bessie.

The only letter from Boucher is the following epistle written from the White Hart in Devizes, where he was staying previous to being fetched away by Mrs Beard on the night of the elopement:

I will marry you when or where you please.

J Boucher.

Crown Court
Abduction at Market Lavington

2nd March 1865

The last case of the Assizes was that of James Boucher, described as a draper, 34 years of age, who was charged with unlawfully taking a young unmarried girl named Catherine Alice Box out of the possession of her father, an engineer at Market Lavington; and Elizabeth Beard, a married woman, who was charged with aiding the abduction. Miss Box is only 15 years old, and the circumstances connected with the abduction, considering her extreme youth, excited considerable interest, the Court being crowded throughout the trial.

Mr Saunders was counsel for the prosecution; Mr H T Cole for the prisoner Boucher, and Mr Prideaux for Mrs Beard.

Mr Saunders said the charge against the two prisoners at the bar was that they abducted from the possession of her father a young girl, unmarried, of the name of Catherine Alice Box, she being at the time of the abduction under 16 years of age. The case was not one of very usual occurrence. However, it sometimes occurred that charges of this kind were properly preferred, and he believed that this case had been prosecuted upon very good and substantial grounds. It was not at all necessary that the abduction should have taken place against the consent of the party abducted; in fact, it was not often that this was so. On the contrary, the party abducted was frequently a willing party to the abduction; and so it was in this case. The object of the law being to defend parents in the proper control of their children when of tender age, and girls themselves against the wiles and villainies of those who wished to gain possession of them. The law therefore was as much for the protection of the girl as for her parents, and it was nothing to the purpose that the girl was a willing party. If it was found that she had been led away by others, those others were guilty, although it might be found that the girl herself was most anxious to leave her home.

The facts were simply these: The parents of the girl are a Mr Box and his wife, respectable people living at Market Lavington. Mr Box is an engineer, the parent of a large family, and the girl in question was his second child, and it appears that for many months prior to the 13th September, the day the abduction took place, she had formed an intimacy with the male prisoner, James Boucher, and this intimacy had been going on for 8 or 9 months. The female prisoner was a Mrs Beard, who had been residing in the same village of Market Lavington, and to whose house the male prisoner and the young woman were in the habit of going. She was aware of the intimacy and the attachment which had sprung up between Miss Box and Boucher, and it was very much at her suggestion that the elopement took place. She was aware of what the young people were going to do, and of the disapprobation which existed on the part of the parents, and she had suggested that they should go to London and get married.

The elopement having been thus previously arranged, on the 13th September the girl retired to her rest at the usual time, and was seen in bed at half past 9 that evening, her father at the time having no suspicion of anything wrong. It appeared however that as soon as all inmates had retired to their rooms, the girl got up, dressed herself, came downstairs with a bundle of clothing in her hands, and was met outside by the male prisoner who was waiting to receive her, and they both then went off to the house of Mrs Beard, who was anticipating their arrival.

Mrs Beard, it would appear, had promised to furnish them with a horse and trap to take them to Woodborough station. However they stayed for some hours with Mrs Beard, and in consequence of the horse having previously fallen down on a journey from Devizes the same evening, they were obliged to walk to the station, and they passed the night at Woodborough.

Early in the morning they proceeded to London by the first train, and on their arrival in town took lodgings near the railway station. Of course, when the girl's absence was discovered, Mr and Mrs Box were in a state of great anxiety, and on searching the bedroom which she had occupied, they discovered on a press a note to the following effect: 'Good-bye. I am gone to Poulshot. Care not for me. I shall be happy. I am going to be married'.

Her father however, on making inquiry, found that instead of going to Poulshot, his daughter had gone to the Woodborough station, and from thence to London, where they were afterwards found together in lodgings near the Paddington Station.

Mr Saunders then proceeded to call the following evidence:

William Box: I am an engineer living at Market Lavington, about 4 and-a-half miles from Devizes. I am a married man with 7 children. One named Catherine Alice is my daughter; she is 15 and-a-half years old. The prisoner Beard resided at Lavington a short time before the elopement. I have seen the prisoner Boucher at Lavington also; I was not aware anything existed between my daughter and Boucher. I went to bed on Tuesday 13th September about 10 o'clock. My daughter was at home and went to bed; the next morning she was missing. I received a note from my wife the next morning; I made enquiries and was informed that my daughter and Boucher had gone to Woodborough. I proceeded there, but could not find any trace of them. I returned and went to London on Wednesday the 14th. When I arrived in London I went to Scotland Yard and made enquiries there. The next day I was informed that the prisoner was in custody at Paddington police station. My daughter was in the care of the officer. The prisoner was brought back to Devizes. It was quite against my will she left.

Cross-examined by Mr Cole: I have three daughters. My daughter Catherine was born on the 22nd of December 1848. I never knew she had a young man. She was never given to going out with young men. I was never aware she was out with the prisoner Boucher. I once turned the prisoner out of my yard neck and crop, because I found him one morning by my kiln fire. I asked him what he wanted. He said, to light his pipe. I told him to do so and go. He did not do so, and I took him by the collar and turned him out, and told him if he came here again I would put him in the water hole. I do not know my daughter was uncomfortable at home. I never spoke to my wife about Boucher. The note written by Miss Box ran thus, 'Mamma is determined I shall not see you'. I ascertained they slept in separate beds. My wife took my daughter to a surgeon. He said she had not been injured.

Sarah Ann Box: I am wife of the last witness and mother of Catherine Alice Box. She is about 15 and-a-half years old. I saw her in bed on Tuesday 13th September last. The next morning she was missing. I found a note in my daughter's handwriting. I did not consent to her leaving home.

Cross-examined by Mr Cole: My daughter occasionally went for a walk. I was always on good terms with her. She never wished to leave home. I was never aware she walked with Boucher. She slept at the back part of the house, some distance from my room. A younger daughter slept with her. I saw them in bed together on the night in question. I was not aware my daughter had any affection for Boucher.

Catherine Alice Box: I am the daughter of the last two witnesses. I had known the prisoner previous to the 13th September about 9 months. I was in the habit of meeting him as a sweetheart. I was also acquainted with Mrs Beard about 2 months before the 13th September. I was going up the street one day and Mrs Beard called me into her house. She asked me if I did not like Mr Boucher. I did not answer her. She said your papa and mamma will not let you see Mr Boucher, will they? I replied no. She said I would if I were you; I would by night if I couldn't by day. She asked me to come up to her house the same evening to see Mr Boucher. She said she would fetch him over. I did not go that night, but 2 nights after, and then saw Mrs Beard and Mr Boucher. I went several times afterwards and generally met Mr Boucher.

A day or two before I left home I was at Mrs Beard's house with Boucher, and it was then agreed that we should go away on that night. I did not however go, because I received a note from Mrs Beard saying Boucher was not coming. Nothing had then been said by Mrs Beard where we were to go. On the Sunday before we had settled on Bath; Mrs Beard said she thought we had better go to Bath instead of to London, and that her brother should take us to the railway station with his horse and trap.

I left home on Tuesday, and on the evening of that day I saw Mrs Beard pass as I was in the sitting room. On her return I was upstairs, at the passage window. She had a white pocket handkerchief, and waving it, she said "Good night! I've got him.". I remained at home until all had gone to bed. About half an hour afterwards I got up and came down with a bundle of clothes, and on going out to the entrance gate I found Mr Boucher. We both of us went to Market Lavington. I went to Mrs Beard's and he went to the Dragon. He afterwards came over to Mrs Beard's and we stayed there till about 1 o'clock. We told her we were going, and she then said that her brother could not drive us as the horse had fallen down. She asked us to write to her directly we got to London. She said we could get married directly we got there.

Whilst I was there that evening, I handed over to her a number of Mr Boucher's letters to me. We burnt her letters to me. She said we'll burn all these letters, so they shan't be seen another day.

On leaving, Mr Boucher and I walked to Woodborough, about 6 miles off, and on arriving there we stayed at a cottage for the night. By the first train in the morning we proceeded to London. I took the tickets and paid for them with Mr Boucher's money. On reaching Paddington, we went to a coffee house, No.1 London Street, and then I wrote to Mrs Beard as I had promised. I and Boucher spent the day going about London, and amongst other places we went to a jeweller's and purchased a wedding ring. The next day (Thursday) Boucher was apprehended by a police officer. I saw my father that day.

Before I left my bedroom on Tuesday night, I wrote on a piece of paper and left it in a place where I thought they would find it, saying that I was gone to Poulshot. Mr Boucher wished me to write it. I had an uncle at Poulshot. The piece of paper contained the words 'Good-bye. I am gone to Poulshot. Don't care about me. I am going to be married'.

Mr Cole: And that was the prevailing wish of your heart?

Miss Box: Yes.

Mr Cole: And you went to London and bought the wedding ring?

Miss Box: Yes, but Mr Boucher paid for it.

Mr Cole: You took all his money, didn't you?

Miss Box: Yes. He said I could have it, and I put it in my purse, but I left him some silver. I took the gold and left him the silver. I first became acquainted with Boucher at Lavington on a Sunday afternoon; the Sunday after Christmas Day, December 1863.

Mr Cole: You got very fond of him, eh?

Miss Box: We got friendly.

Mr Cole: Did you get so friendly that you soon were in the habit of meeting him at night. Kissing acquaintance, eh? 'My own dearest Jim', eh? Was not that the style? Come, Miss Box.

Miss Box said nothing.

Mr Cole: Well I suppose silence with a lady gives consent. Well, didn't you use to write to him 4 times a day? Didn't you write thus: 'Dear Jim, this is the fourth time today, and unless you are sober, and I hear you are worse today, I shall come tonight and tell you what I mean'.

Miss Box admitted that she had done so; that she had met him at 4 o'clock in the morning, that she had written to him telling him a walk would do him good these summer mornings, and that she was so shamefully treated at home that she could not stand it. She did not know how she had come to write that. The remainder of the letter ran thus: 'I would rather die than remain here miserable and be unable to see you. If I could see you every day I should be as happy as a lark. My home would then be a most joyous one; now most unhappy'.

Mr Cole: Was not this to induce the man to go away and marry you?

Miss Box: He always wished me to go. My parents were never unkind to me. I used to write to Boucher to meet me at 4 in the morning.

Mr Cole then read another letter addressed to Boucher:

Dearest one:

will you, dear Jim, favour me with your company tomorrow morning at 4 o'clock. I know you will come if you can. Accept sweetest love and kisses, from her who forgets the past and loves dearer than before.

From yours, ever dearest as before Alice.

Miss Box: I do not think I met him 100 times during the 9 months. I never wrote to a man named Titchborne; I never used to walk with young Dowse, or a young man named Cooper; my sister walked with Cooper, and my sister introduced Boucher to me, but she did not know I was meeting him. Boucher was a little the worse for liquor the night we went away. I carried the bundle to Erchfont, and then a person was engaged to carry it on. We were to have been married on Friday morning, but unluckily the policeman came.

After reading another letter written in a similar strain to the preceding ones, Mr Cole sat down, and Miss Box was then subjected to the cross-examination of Mr Prideaux, and in answer to him she said she used to meet Boucher at Mehila's, a washerwoman. She wrote a letter appointing to meet there at eleven o'clock one night, signed, 'Believe me, with a love and a kiss, yours ever, Kate Box'. She had then met Boucher only twice before.

Miss Box: I did not ask Mrs Beard the first time I went to her house if she knew Boucher. I did not say he's a nice man. Mrs Beard did not say 'he's not a man I should admire', but the evening before we went away she told me she should never like him. She never advised me not to have him; never until the Monday when she wrote me, but then she fetched him. I did say to Mrs Beard 'no more is your husband one that I should admire'. Mrs Beard did not say to me the best thing you can do is to tell your mother. I did not ask Mrs Beard whether I had better not wear slack jackets 'to hide it'.

I know Mary Jane Hampton and Jane Merrett. I did not in their presence ask Mrs Beard whether I had not better wear slack jackets to hide my getting large. Mrs Beard did not, in the presence of those persons, tell me the best thing I could do was to tell my mother. I recollect Mrs Beard remarking that I was very young. I did not reply I shall be 19 next December and the Princess was married at 18. Boucher was often drunk. I remember on one occasion his being locked up and fined. Mrs Beard did not advise me to have nothing to do with him in consequence of his drunken habits. She never tried to dissuade me.

Miss Box admitted that she wrote a letter to Mrs Beard saying: 'Do not be so determined; let your brother drive us to the station'. She wrote this because Mrs Beard had previously said that if she was afterwards found to have had anything to do with it she should get into trouble.

Miss Box: Mrs Beard said that she wished me not to go, to which I replied in a letter, 'I am determined; if he will, I will; or I will tell everything'.

In another letter to Mrs Beard, Miss Box said:

Mrs Dyke has reported a tale about me. She may say what she likes; if it is true I can't help it. I wish he would have me. I see no prospect of happiness without him. I love him, and always shall do.

Miss Box: Mr Boucher had previously told me that Mrs Dyke had reported that I was in the family way. I did write another letter to Mr Boucher in which I said: 'Mrs Farmer has said that I am in **** guess what? Is it not a lie? I know Mamma has her suspicion'. But this referred to my speaking to Boucher. Yes I wrote another letter, commencing 'Dearest Bessie, do let your brother drive us to Woodborough station Monday night. I will do anything in return. Jim is afraid to ask Mr House as he may say no, and tell all. If you will not have anything to do with our going, I must arrange all'. So that I was determined to go, if I walked.

Another letter to Mrs Beard read:

Dearest Bessie,

I write this little scribble to tell you I have good news of this morning. He is coming over to pay you the little bill he owes you. Then we are off to town. So that if you are determined to have nothing to do with our going, which I think is not very kind, I am determined to walk.

Miss Box: The night we went to Woodborough station I did not go to Mrs Beard's, and finding Boucher there, say 'Who would have thought of seeing you here? I heard your voice at the Dragon'. Mr Boucher was drunk at this time. Mrs Merrett was there. I went away with her and her little boy. I did not say to her when I parted, 'Good-bye; I may never see you again; I am going to Poulshot'. I waited until Mrs Merrett was out of sight, and then came back to Mrs Beard's. When Mrs Beard went by our house and waved a handkerchief, I opened the staircase window, and heard her say, 'I've got him'. I had been expecting her to return, and that was the reason I looked out. It was a very moonlight night. Father and Mother were at this time in the sitting room below. I heard Mrs Beard say distinctly, 'Good night; come up; I've got him'. I heard 'come up' quite plain, and 'got him' quite plain.

A great deal more of cross-examination followed, with the view of exculpating Mrs Beard, and Miss Box was then released from the witness box.

The policeman who took Boucher into custody in London was next examined, and also Superintendent Wolfe, who said that on going to the house of Mrs Beard at Market Lavington, Mrs Beard told him that Miss Box and Boucher were at her house only 10 minutes on the night of their elopement, and that she had turned Miss Box out of doors and sent her home, and that her husband had turned Boucher out of doors. She accounted for fetching Boucher from Devizes by saying that he owed her husband some money, and that as soon as they had got it out of him they turned him out of doors. Mr Wolfe however produced a number of letters, which put rather a different construction upon Mrs Beard's motives.

This was the case for the prosecution.

Mr Cole then asked his lordship whether he considered there was any case to go to the jury.

The judge briefly referred to two or three points in the case, more particularly to the evidence given by Miss Box, many parts of which he considered very unsatisfactory.

Addressing himself to the jury, he said: "I don't know, gentlemen, whether you would wish to hear the evidence on the part of the defence, or whether you are satisfied that the case is not sufficiently made out by the prosecution."

One of the jurymen replied, "We don't wish to hear the defence."

Upon this, his lordship made some further remarks with reference to Boucher, who he said, might probably in a half drunken state, have been drawn into it by other parties. If however the jury wished to hear any portion of the defence, he was quite ready to go on.

Several of the jury said they were satisfied that there was not sufficient evidence on which they could return a verdict of guilty against either of the prisoners, and both Boucher and Mrs Beard were consequently at once discharged.

The verdict was received by the audience with applause and clapping of hands. No sooner was Boucher outside the Court than another lusty cheer was given for him, and he walked off like a man who fancies himself a hero or a martyr, it is difficult to say which, perhaps both.

16th March 1865

James Minor was summoned by Mr Box of Market Lavington for leaving his service on the 6th March. Before the case was gone into, Mr Box said he wished to make the same offer to the defendant he had previously made, viz., that if he would apologize for his misconduct, pay the costs and return to work, he would proceed no further. At the same time he handed a written agreement between himself and Minor to the Bench, by which agreement it appeared that Minor was bound to serve Mr Box at 10s a week from January to December 1865.

The Bench, having read the agreement, persuaded Minor to accede to Mr Box's offer, but this he refused to do, and the case accordingly proceeded. It transpired that Minor was one of the principal witnesses on behalf of Mrs Beard in the late Market Lavington abduction case. He was on that occasion absent 3 days, but it was not on account of these 3 days that Mr Box complained. It was for having absented himself for 2 days after the trial, and as the absence could not be defended, Minor at last very reluctantly consented, after having been informed that he had rendered himself liable to 3 months imprisonment, to apologize, pay the expenses, and return to his work.

(Catharine Box married Walter William Smith, a journeyman carpenter from Market Lavington in 1869, when she was 20 years old. The couple had 2 daughters: Beatrice, born in 1869, and Mary, born at the end of 1870. In April 1871, Walter travelled to America aboard 'The City of London', and declared his occupation as a farmer. Later that year, Catharine and her 2 daughters, along with her younger brother Alfred, boarded the same ship from Liverpool and joined her husband for a new life in the United States.

Bessie Beard was Elizabeth Hampton, born in Potterne in 1842. At the time of the abduction she was only 23 years of age, and had been married to John Beard for 2 years. There doesn't appear to have been any pecuniary interest for her in this abduction, so it is possible she was involved from a misplaced interest in aiding romance).

INDEX

House	54, 116, 117, 122, 126, 128, 137
Hulbert	21, 36
Ingram	15,
Jackson	37,
Jenkinson	32,
Joliffe	47,
Kelsey	19, 25, 28, 36, 45, 65, 72
Kenningham	35,
King	45,
Kite, Kyte	18, 19, 67, 68, 69, 70, 96, 97
Lambert	28,
Lane	11, 99
Langdon	36,
Langley	91,
Lawes	28, 49
Lennard	49, 93, 95, 96
Littlewood	37,
Locke	123,
Long	85,
Loyd	25,
Ludlow	63,
Lush	28, 44, 45, 46, 47, 56, 97,98
Lye	45,
Mansfield	121,
Martin	122, 128
Maslen	32,
Mayow	28,
Mead	45, 47, 91
Meredith	66, 71
Merrett	45, 46, 136, 138
Merriman	36,
Minor	140,

Moule	85,
Neate	24, 25, 44, 46, 54, 55, 57
Newman	24, 28, 33, 52, 92
Nichols	37,
Nixon	17,
Noad	26,
Nosworthy	45,
Nutland	23,
Oatley	72,
Olivier	78,
Patten	91,
Pearless	55,
Pearson	36, 37
Pepler	40, 103, 107, 108, 109, 112
Phillips	23, 94
Philpot	85,
Phipp, Phipps	48, 78
Plank	90,
Pomeroy	45,
Potter	23, 40
Powell	17,
Price	36,
Prideaux	129, 136
Radnor	13,
Read	104,
Rimer	54,
Robbins	45,
Rowbottom	45, 47
Rumble	21, 90, 91
Sainsbury	28, 29, 30, 36, 45, 49, 50,
Sainsbury	56, 63, 80, 87, 88, 90
Saunders	14, 15, 43, 83, 84, 85, 88,
Saunders	129, 131

Made in the USA
Charleston, SC
29 November 2012